BABY BOOMERS' GUIDE TO WEALTH AND INVESTING

JOHN ST. CROIX

UPHILL PUBLISHING LTD.

Published in 1997 by
Uphill Publishing Ltd.
190 Attwell Drive
Suite 400
Toronto, Ontario
M9W 6H8

First printing May 1997

John St. Croix, 1961 -
The Baby Boomers' Guide To Wealth And Investing

ISBN 0-9698432-9-1
1. Finance, Personal - Canada.
2. Tax Planning - Canada.
3. Retirement - Canada - Planning.
I. Title
HG179.S24 1997 332.024'00971 C97-930328-1

Illustrations: Steven Nease
Printer: Gladding Graphics Ltd.
Printed in Canada

Dedication

To my beautiful wife Tracy, and our three wonderful daughters, Margeaux, Abby and Brooke, for their ongoing love and support.

TABLE OF CONTENTS:

INTRODUCTION: THE BABY BOOMERS' GUIDE TO WEALTH & INVESTING.

BY: JOHN ST. CROIX

The Toronto Blue Jays are twenty years old. M*A*S*H has been off the air for 13 years. John Lennon was assassinated on December 8, 1980, seventeen years ago. On September 28, 1997, Canadians will celebrate the twenty-fifth anniversary of Paul Henderson's winning goal in the 1972 Canada-Russia series! On April 6, 1996, an article in *The Globe & Mail* entitled "Growing old is a baby booming business," warned anyone, including authors, from reminding Boomers of our age. In the article, University of Toronto professor David Foot, author of *Boom, Bust & Echo*, states: "We all think that we are ten years younger than we really are. If you're going to market to an aging workplace...you don't confront people with their age." Further in the article, Tom Akins, president of AgeSpeak of Kansas City, Mo., a consulting firm that specializes in our changing demographics, confirms this fact. He says, "Boomers do tend to think of themselves as younger. They don't think of themselves as looking the age they are." That said, why would this author and financial advisor who is marketing services to Baby Boomers, do just that? Why would I confront the Boomers with age and, more specifically, with the idea that "time flies"? The simple answer, I must.

I am not in the fashion business. My job is not to create seamless bifocals for glasses, to tell you how great that you look in your Lexus or to help you lose weight so that you may enjoy all of the newest clothing styles. My job is to prepare you for retirement. Statistics state that your retirement could last two, ten or even forty years! This means that you may not require very much money when your income stops, or you may need a great deal. To this, add an inflation factor over thirty or forty years and a shockingly astronomical amount may be necessary. Many Boomers have just recently discovered R.R.S.P.'s and in some cases are poorly invested there. This means that many are either taking too much risk to "catch up" or, out of fear and a lack of knowledge, they have positioned themselves too conservatively and will ultimately lose to inflation. Many of us have come to the realization that government pensions and, in an increasing number of cases even company pensions, are "shaky at best". As some of you read this, you may say; "Ah but John doesn't realize that I work for XYZ CORPORATION and that we have one of the finest benefit and retirement plans in Canada." Most entrepreneurs understand going in that they will be 100% responsible for building a personal retirement plan. In addition, many self-employed individuals have built "saleable" equity in a company that can be liquidated in whole or in part at retirement. This is why entrepreneurs, in my opinion, have the best chance of becoming the long-term millionaires of tomorrow. It has to work like that. The owners of the company get rich while the workers tend to be at the owner's mercy, particularly over the long term. Why, because things change. If you don't believe me, leave XYZ CORPORATION for an afternoon and ask one of the seven thousand workers over at ABCD CORP., also once a big company, how they feel about being part of the "rightsizing" campaign of their company. Do you think that the majority of these individuals were fully prepared to "retire early"? Are you?

Does this type of talk concern you? Does it make you feel uneasy or scare you?! I am concerned about those people who do not take it seriously. As a financial advisor, individuals and couples of the Baby Boom Generation come into my office all the time; some have done an outstanding job of both saving and investing effectively. A second group is justifiably concerned because they have not started or become serious about saving for retirement. The largest group of Boomers though, are those people who are serious about retirement. These people have paid down a mortgage and are real savers, however, their problem lies with what they do with their savings. They do not have a professional financial advisor or a solid plan in place to retire. Furthermore, they do not understand how much money they will actually need to retire or, at their present pace of savings, what type of rate of return will be required (not just desired) to achieve their retirement goals. In short, their heart is in the right place, but they need to adjust their personal investment philosophy in order to make their long term goals become a reality. To do this, knowledge through education, backed up by the application of that knowledge is necessary. This is where I come in.

I believe that the role of today's financial advisor has changed. Over the past several years (almost eleven in my case), the investment landscape and the advisor-client relationship has evolved. Initially in my career, my job was simply to "invest people's money". By around 1990, I shifted my focus, as many financial advisors did, to a far more consultative role. In other words, advisors became fully involved in their clients' goals. Indeed, "client service" became the watchword of most businesses and financial planning was no exception. Competition also began to heat up and investors began to exercise their choices with respect to switching investment firms, investment products and financial advisors. Presently, I believe that the advisor-client relationship is cemented by three distinct criteria:

1. Outstanding and timely advice, as well as excellent client service.

2. Low cost, coupled with strong and highly competitive returns.

3. Education, so that the advisor and the client can actually work together and so that only a reasonable and comfortable amount of trust is given to the advisor.

Considering the importance of these three areas, let's examine them further:

Advice And Service:

Simply put, this is the consistency of contact and the strength of the investors relationship with an advisor. The commitment on the advisor's part must be to keep up with each individual client and their changing needs and situations. This may involve an upcoming retirement, a change in jobs, a death in the family that impacts upon the financial status, either positively or negatively, separation and divorce or a host of other material financial changes. Another commitment lies with your advisor in respect to his/her willingness to stay abreast of changes in the investment climate and to assist you in using those changes to your best advantage rather than allowing change to pass you by.

Low Cost And Competitive Returns:

In my career, I have come across many clients who have achieved a strong rate of return only to promptly (and sometimes unwittingly) give it back to an advisor in the form of unnecessary commissions. Clients today are cognizant of their costs in investing. The objective has to be to keep costs to the client low and achieve strong profitability within our own individual practices.

This clearly works under the business guidelines of a "win-win" situation for everyone involved. An absence of high cost to an investor is not enough. Because Baby Boomers are faced with some daunting retirement goals, strong results are needed. In many cases, they are investing "for free", but receiving no advice and some dismal returns. If your investments are not competitive with others in their investment class, then whatever your financial objectives are, they are just that much further away! For example, in mutual funds, there are Canadian equity funds with a five year average, annual, compound return of 20% per year. Other funds have a return of 4.5% in the same category for that identical time period. The frightening part is that the lesser company does not advertise poor performance and as such, you have to discern this for yourself or through your advisor. Another factor in respect to "competitive returns" has to do with a false sense of security in good years. For example, someone states proudly; "my Canadian equity fund did 11.5% last year!" Well, that is excellent, unless the average of all Canadian equity funds was 17.4% and if 20 of these funds performed over 20%! In this case, a lack of preparation or homework has clearly put you at a disadvantage. So then, the key for all investors (and specifically Baby Boomers) is to achieve strong returns and to not be seduced by the "sex appeal" of trading yourself into negative returns or depleting your returns through unnecessary impatience.

Education:

I trust my Doctor, however, not to the point where she recommends an operation that I do not even remotely understand, particularly if one of my children is involved! Many of us have become very familiar with health issues today. The financial industry is not any different. When a forty-five year old is faced with building up $700,000 over the next fifteen years for retirement, then that person or couple usually becomes very interested in the "how to" element attached to that task. A financial advisor's task is to give you definitive answers in this case. This comes in the form of individual meetings, quarterly newsletters, seminars and recommended reading. This type of environment is not designed to turn an investor into a financial advisor. Instead, education builds trust and both the advisor and the client work from the same page.

All of these factors equal one paramount attitudinal position for the Baby Boomer who is serious about financial success; that is of course, self reliance. That is the theme of this book. It is about taking control of your financial life, once and for all! To achieve this, take the following steps:

1. Do not depend solely on the government or your present employer.

2. Build a strong, long-term relationship with an outstanding financial advisor.

3. Achieve excellent, competitive returns that will allow you to reach your financial goals.

4. Continue to learn. Knowledge is power, and in the area of investing it is becoming more of a necessity than just an everyday desire.

My experience with many Baby Boomers has been such that they know that they have to do something, but in some cases it has been put off for so long that they do not know how to start; and/or they do not want to hear that they "may be in trouble financially". In most cases, a financial plan remedies their situation and consistently leaves them with a feeling of: "Why didn't we do this sooner? It was painless!" The mind-set then, must be to face your task head-on and "fear not!" A lump in a woman's breast, if caught early enough can save her life. If ignored, it may cost her her life. Similarly, don't start planning your future the day after your company announces a plan to "down-size". Start today, and as you plan, educate and implement a powerful program of building wealth, it will alter your future in a way you had never imagined possible. Indeed, the world of compound interest awaits, but self-reliance is the key to entering that remarkable world. Enjoy the book and put into practice what you will learn. That is my advice.

"People never plan to be failures; they simply fail to plan to be successful."

William A. Ward.

CHAPTER 1

WHAT THE BABY BOOMERS WANT TO KNOW

No, this chapter does not have anything to do with world peace, a clean environment or a cure for hair loss! Although those issues are very important, this is a financial book. What I would like to first examine is what is important to Baby Boomers, financially speaking, now and in the future. First though, I should establish, who is a Baby Boomer? The typical person that comes to mind is the forty-three year old computer analyst, married with four children who is conservative by all accounts during waking hours. When the kids are asleep, however, the analyst and his/her spouse head down to the basement, put on the headphones and listen to "The Doors" or "Iron Butterfly" on volume ten of their stereo! Although I am stereotyping with this example, in reality a Baby Boomer is anyone who was born between 1946 and

1966. That means 30 year olds to 50 year olds are Boomers. I was born on December 21, 1961, so I am a Baby Boomer, albeit on the back end of the scale. I personally associate the Boomers with someone in my oldest brother's age group: Steve is forty-two. If you remember in my introduction, I stated that Boomers like to think of themselves as younger than they actually are. Thus, Steve likes to think of himself as twenty-two. That is perfectly fine with me because Steve is seven years older than I am, therefore I can occasionally act fifteen. Anyhow, if you are a Boomer, this chapter will probably have some strong significance to past discussions you have had concerning your financial objectives.

Over the past ten years, I have had the pleasure of having long, fascinating discussions with investors about their financial objectives. This area of financial planning is far and away the most personal and, arguably, the most important. This is the time when people tell their advisor about their financial fears, dreams and aspirations for their personal future. It is through these years of interview notes, as well as through discussions with other financial advisors and, finally, using "random interviews" with Baby Boomers that I have compiled a comprehensive list of what the Boomers want to know. Their concerns and questions are varied. However, four or five areas are consistent. They include:

1. How much money will we actually need at retirement?

2. What is the most effective way for us to build up a retirement plan, keeping pace with inflation, yet allowing us to sleep at night?

3. How will we ever be able to afford our children's education?

4. I would like to start my own business. What type of capital will I need?

5. Please, help us save tax!

Other areas that also come up fairly regularly are:

1. What steps can we take to get out of debt?

2. We are concerned about job security. Are there any measures that we can personally take financially to protect ourselves?

3. What is the best way to stop living "pay to pay?"

4. How do we build an "emergency fund?" Also, how much should it be?

5. How much and what type of life insurance coverage do we need?

6. Should we invest in stocks?

7. What should our "asset mix" of fixed income to equities be?

8. How should we choose mutual funds?

9. What are the advantages of no-load versus load mutual funds?

10. Are labour sponsored funds effective?

11. We have heard a great deal about borrowing to invest. Is this a strategy we should consider?

12. How can we pay off our mortgage early?

13. What is the best and safest way for our parents to invest?

14. How do we choose a financial advisor?

15. What steps can we take to learn about investing, short of taking the Canadian Securities course?

16. When should we sell an investment?

17. We are concerned about the future of Canada both from a standpoint of unity and debt accumulation. How concerned should we be and how should this effect our investment decisions.

Do a couple of these sound familiar? If you have taken the time to consider financial planning, either on your own, as a couple, or with a professional financial advisor, some or several of these questions and concerns have most likely been examined. Some areas are of more concern than others, however; that depends solely on the individual investor. For the purposes of our book, let's look a little further into the most common concerns. They are as follows:

Retirement Planning: How Much Will I Need? How Should I Build Money While Employing Safety And Inflation Protection?

We will look at these issues in much greater detail later on in the book. For now though, I would like to expand on retirement planning as it relates to what the Baby Boomers want. Once an individual or couple fully retires, that is to say, strolls into the personnel office and gives notice (or for entrepreneurs, decides to sell their company), there is "no going back." This is one of the most unnerving aspects of retirement. It has been my experience in retirement planning that individuals and couples agonize over the "timing of their retirement," particularly in the last two or three years of their working life. In the actual months leading up to retirement, the tension in the investor's life can be excruciating! In speaking with people who did take that step and are actually retired, this tension comes from two overriding and constant thoughts leading up to retirement. The first one is universal and very often talked about openly: "Do we have enough money?" Most people have looked at their financial needs and those needs may be adequately met, at least in the initial stages of retirement.

There is of course a "wild card" in retirement: the variable amount of inflation. This amount, if high enough, will destroy a retiree's purchasing power which, in its most rudimentary and most personal form, means that you will not live as well in the future as you are living today. Consequently, a financial plan, established prior to retiring, should include:

1. Realistic income expectations.

2. A long term inflation hedging portion to the investment portfolio.

3. A knowledge of the expected returns and risks of various investments that can be used for growth and income.

4. An understanding of estate planning.

5. A tax advantageous element where possible.

In addition, the pre-retirement plan should be personal in recognizing the special needs of the individual investor. Once the question of "sufficient retirement funding" is answered by your financial advisor, the second area of pre-retirement tension should be addressed. This second concern is much more personal and far less talked about than the first: the notion of "productivity". Indeed, only as a couple or through a close friend will you come to terms with what to do with all of your free time. Today's worker is very busy and extremely productive.

Many Baby Boomers put in fifty or sixty hour work weeks. In retirement the work week for which you are actually responsible may equal zero and for many this is a frightening prospect! The good news is that the vast majority of retirees, in my experience, are very productive; but in their own way and on their own terms. Retirement, if the health and wealth aspects are in place, should be a "second coming of your teenage years." Many retirees whom I know, are constantly euphoric in the knowledge that this is their time to enjoy. In addition, retirees are usually extremely confident, after all, they've lived! This means that they are past issues such as "keeping up with the Jones'". They have more free time to read or learn about computers, politics, sports and the like. Many have improved their golf games threefold. All of this makes for a very interesting and extremely productive individual. Thus, in pre-retirement planning, I recommend not just a plan, but perhaps a few interviews with some people who have been retired for a while. The knowledge gained here may quell your fears.

For the present day Baby Boomer, another pre-retirement planning issue is: "How to invest for safety and protect against inflation." For me, as a financial advisor, these aspects represent the same thing. Let me explain: "safety" is a relative term and to many people, "safety" means "guaranteed". As I stated in my first book, *Tips From The Top*, this form of safety is actually artificial, for although it recognizes a predetermined rate of return, in many cases, these "safe" investments fail to address the nemesis of long-term inflation. The investment concern of the Boomers, however, is very real with respect to striking a balance between long-term, powerful and meaningful growth on your investments; and "the pillow factor": your ability to sleep at night. Throughout the book I will show you how to build this balance.

How Will We Afford Our Children's Education?

Funding education is another cocktail party favourite of the Baby Boomers, at least at the boring "financial advisor parties" I attend. Later in the book we will devote a chapter to this issue. Right now though, we are pondering why Boomers find these particular issues so important. Indeed, as parents most people are extremely unselfish, moreover, they want to see their children succeed. As a parent, permit me to speak for all of us: we want our kids to have at least the same advantages that we were afforded. One fact is certain: in most cases, the Baby Boomers were afforded "the luxury" of education and it was "a choice" whether or not to take advantage of that opportunity. The fear of today's Boomer is that our kids may lose that "choice"; thus it is our desire to assist in any way possible.

I Have A Great Business Idea! How Much Money Will I Need?

As an entrepreneur myself, I love other entrepreneurs. Indeed, it takes a great deal of self-confidence to determine your own worth. However, as we see in the paper, bankruptcies are everywhere and people are failing! The upside to this is that people are also succeeding and, in many cases, they are succeeding "big"! The Baby Boomers are a major component of that entrepreneurial success. We have learned, sometimes the hard way, that depending on ourselves and our own abilities is, in fact, the greatest form of security. I have been in business for over ten years and I have yet to fire myself. All that said, going into a business opportunity with a positive attitude, but naive, can be a formula for disaster. Depending on the business opportunity, there are usually some start up costs.

You must determine the equipment needed, office space, staff, marketing costs, outside consulting fees, such as lawyers and accountants, and at the same time have the ability to withstand periods of time with little or no income. Ultimately, when a business is in the initial stages, one should be able to go twelve to eighteen months without drawing a salary.

How Can We Consistently Save Tax?

Why is the tax issue important to Baby Boomers? My interviews with clients have revealed three reasons:

1. In many cases Boomers are in their prime earning years and most are in the highest tax brackets.

2. Thus, we are paying gigantic amounts of income tax each and every year with no end in sight.

3. In many provinces, the combined federal and provincial tax rate at its highest (and most disgusting) level

exceeds fifty percent!!! Moreover, there is a general feeling of "What are we getting for this type of money"?

4. It does not take Stephen Hawking to figure out that the more money you give to the government, the less that is available for you to build for retirement, children's educations, holidays, new golf clubs, the Harley Davidson that you have not yet told your wife about; and a plethora of other uses for the money the government takes.

Each person's financial goals are unique and personal. However, the Baby Boomers have spoken. They are concerned about many important financial issues and although the challenges for Boomers are great they are equal to the task. I state this with confidence, in the face of our ever changing planet. With tremendous change comes tremendous opportunity for personal and financial growth. My experience with many Boomers, be they clients or friends, is nothing short of inspiring. Indeed, Boomers are smart and, even more importantly, they are aware. This is not a society of people who have their "heads in the sand"; Boomers talk about financial issues openly and intelligently. It is this attitude of both information gathering, as well as its actual application through investment that will position the Baby Boomers in a comfortable position as we move into the new millennium. I look forward to being a part of this movement. Finally, facing issues and concerns head-on is fast becoming a way of life for the Boomer;

and the movement towards self-reliance and self-confidence coupled with co-operation is in evidence.

Now that we have established what the Baby Boomers want to know, let's go forward to determine just how to make those dreams and goals a reality. Each of us has hopes and aspirations for ourselves and for our children's futures. However, we will face large and unexpected financial and personal obstacles along the way. Understanding this, the only course of action will be to adjust your financial plan and continue to move ahead, impervious to the situations that threaten financial independence. This is the ongoing challenge of the financially ambitious Baby Boomer.

"The nose of the bulldog has been slanted backwards so that he can breathe without letting go."

Winston Churchill.

CHAPTER 2

WHY ARE WE AFRAID? FOR MANY GOOD REASONS!

I see it first-hand every day: Baby Boomers, from all walks of life, with a look of concern or even fear in their eyes. They have either just attended a financial planning seminar, read a pre-retirement book or spoke to a knowledgeable friend. Indeed, setting in is the reality of an unplanned, neglected and dismal retirement. First comes shock, then denial, then comes outright fear. I have heard it described in financial planning circles as "The Charles Dickens" or "Christmas Carol" syndrome. This of course refers to someone pointing out a future of financial hardship and strife, looking at mistakes and neglects of the financial past; and identifying lost opportunities. Then the Boomer is struck by a fear similar to Scrooge's on Christmas morning: Is it too late? Financially speaking, what can we do to change the course of our future?

George Washington said, "To be prepared for war is one of the most effectual means of preserving peace."

Although retirement planning is a far cry from war, Washington's message is appropriate with respect to alleviating the fear we associate with reaching financial goals. How do you break through the initial apprehension of planning for your financial future? Make a plan. In fact, overplan: educate yourself through books, seminars and meetings with your financial advisor. With respect to projecting retirement needs and potential rates of return, be very conservative. Start by using a higher percentage than what is normal today for gauging inflation, add money into your retirement plan that will compensate for "extras" rather than planning for the essentials; and do not allow any advisor to use extremely high rates of return when projecting future returns. Each projection should also be backed up by logical information such as past performance of an investment; and future prospects for the security or mutual fund. In other words, with respect to financial planning, being extremely prepared for the worst will make actual obstacles seem uneventful.

Throughout this book, your knowledge will build and if these ideas are applied into actual investment strategies, then your fear of starting or moving ahead from where you presently are will dissipate. For now though, let's examine why Baby Boomers are concerned about their financial future. To illustrate the task at hand, I would like to show you just one out of many possible common scenarios with respect to what is ahead for the Boomers.

Case 1: Jim And Amanda

Jim: Age 44
Middle Manager in a small manufacturing company.
Annual Income of $58,000.
No pension plan.

Amanda: Age 41
Part time dental hygienist.
Annual income of $32,000.
No pension plan.

Other considerations:
2 children. (Peter age 16, Craig age 13.)
No Mortgage.
Good savers with an excellent commitment to their financial goals.
Amanda is an outstanding "budgeter" and is very interested in learning more about investing. (She has just read *Tips From The Top*.)

Financial Goals

1. As both sons are excellent students with good marks, university or college is in their future. Jim and Amanda would like to make certain that they can provide for the cost of their sons' education. Moreover, they will encourage both boys to live at home during post secondary education years.

2. Retirement is a big priority in both Jim and Amanda's life. As they put it, "we'd like to get back to traveling and making time for ourselves". Together, they figured out that to live comfortably, considering both sons will be out of the nest by then, they will need approximately 70% of their present gross yearly income. Finally, they want this sum to be achieved in 1997 dollars and wish to keep pace with inflation, leading up to and during retirement.

The sum they came up with was $63,000/year, split evenly between them ($31,500 each), and a 4% inflation factor was arbitrarily selected. Jim and Amanda would like to retire in eighteen years, when Jim is sixty-two years old.

Jim And Amanda's Financial Position

Assets:

Cash on hand	$ 4,200
Home, mortgage free	$185,000
Canada Savings Bonds (sons' education)	$ 12,675

RRSPs:

Jim: Mutual funds, Provincial Bonds, GICs
$ 68,431
(average return over last 5 years = 9.2%)

Amanda: GICs, Mutual Funds $ 42,600
(average return over last 5 years = 8.3%)

Miscellaneous Assets:
(Not usable for financial goals) $ 44,000

NO DEBT

Usual yearly savings:
two educations = $6,000/year.
Retirement plan = $8,000/year.

What Jim and Amanda Will Need To Accumulate To Make Their Dreams a Reality

Goal # 1:

Education plan: According to several recent studies and articles published in national newspapers, yearly costs for a "stay-at-home student" are: $6,000 to $6,500 per year in 1997.

Using Our Arbitrary 4% Inflation Factor:

Peter age 16,	
Yearly cost at 4% inflation per year in 2 years	= $ 7,035
Year 2 of university @ 4%	= $ 7,315
Year 3 of university @ 4%	= $ 7,605
Year 4 of university @ 4%	= $ 7,910

Peter's four year educational costs
= $ 29,865

Craig is 13 years old and in 5 years, at age 18, he may enter college or university.

Using our inflation factor of 4%, his first year costs may balloon from $6,500 in 1997 dollars to $7,910 in year 1 of post secondary school. Using the same calculation as Peter's, Craig's total cost for a four year, (live-at-home) education will be a whopping $33,600!

Overall sum to make these Boomers' dream of "educating their children" a reality will be approximately $63,465.

** Please note: For this calculation, I have generously used a 4% inflation factor. As you will read in a later chapter some educators believe that "educational inflation" could be as high as 8 to 10% per year!

Goal # 2:

A comfortable retirement at age sixty-two (using Jim's age) with 70% of their present income coming from investments. This represents $63,000 per year, ($31,500 each) in 1997 dollars.

Again, using our 4% inflation factor, the task is as follows:

1. How much income will we need in 18 years to live as $63,000 earners live today?

   $63,000 @ 4% inflation for 18 years = X

   X = $63,000 x 2.026 = $127,638 per year in 18 years.

2. How large should my lump sum be in order to generate $127,000 per year in retirement without encroaching on my capital?

In this case, I use an 8% retirement income. In other words, your large lump sum should generate an 8% income consistently without long term injury to your principle in retirement.

Example: If you had a lump sum of $1,600,000 (yes, you read it correctly), you could generate the following income:

$1.6 Million x 8% income = $128,000 yearly.

Again, this represents 70% of the lifestyle that Jim and Amanda enjoy today!

3. Another variable in retirement: Inflation during a potential 30 year life of retirement.

What type of monetary provision should we make for that?

A lump sum of $200,000 to $250,000 that is growing indefinitely for the purpose of injecting income into your portfolio would be necessary as you move forward. The reason is clear. Just as $128,000 is needed in 18 short years to live as $63,000 per year earners (to 1997 standards), you will need a continuous upgrade in income during retirement over 30 years or more.

Thus, as a retirement goal, Jim and Amanda will need approximately $1.85 million!!!

So, why are we afraid? In the case of Jim and Amanda, almost $2,000,000 must be built up over the next 2 to 18 years to reach a couple of important financial goals we might take for granted. With government cutbacks, downsizing and the constant threat of higher interest rates and inflation, we need to invest consistently and wisely. As we know, $63,000 per year in 1997 dollars is not living "high on the hog" so to speak. Take a close look at your lifestyle. If you have a relatively high standard of living and you would like to maintain it throughout retirement, investing is not to be taken lightly. Some Boomers will have to significantly lower their retirement income standards, others will sacrifice now for a better financial future; the rest will buy a whole bunch of lottery tickets, and pray.

Do not be discouraged. There is hope and that is why you purchased this book. Read on and let us work together to make sense of this seemingly complex world of investing. You will find, as many investors before you have already learned, that it is not as tough as it seems to be financially independent, however, you must make a commitment to yourself.

CHAPTER 3

STARTING WITHOUT INTIMIDATION

Do you remember the first day you joined a fitness club? I certainly do. Like most of you, it was January 2nd a few years back. I had just finished "pigging out" for a month solid and I made the decision that I do enjoy food immensely, however, I do not like being soft, sluggish and tired looking. My solution was to go out and purchase a pair of $200 Nike's, a gym bag; and all of the gear necessary to "look the part". I then proceeded to the local fitness club to pay my money and (to my mind), ceremoniously "receive my new body". As we know, it doesn't exactly work that way. Two or three visits to the club, some serious pain in muscles I had long forgotten I had, and a ridiculous amount of sweat brought me back to reality. Something else brought me back to reality as well; the "bodies" at the club, particularly of those individuals who had made the decision that I had made, months or even years earlier. These people were in shape and not only looked the part, but could back it up by playing an hour of squash without a break or working out on the "Stairmaster" for 70 minutes; and other feats which, at the time, would have intimidated any beginner and perhaps even given one an inferiority complex. I remember thinking, "Two days ago I was pumped". I was going to get into incredible condition, my wife was going to be impressed; and here I am today wearing $200 shoes, standing beside a twenty year-old guy and a 24 year old lady who look as if they are the children of Arnold and Jackie Joyner Kersey. Heck, it's difficult at first not to be intimidated! However, if you have a goal that is important enough, such as superior, long term health or the prospect of building wealth for yourself and for your family, then you persevere. Whether it be fitness or investing, the shift in the personal thought process can be very similar. At first, you get excited and you want to become rich, you then begin to understand the reality that it will not happen overnight. You also begin to recognize that there are virtually thousands of possible investment choices and that the wrong choices will actually have an inverse effect on your personal economics. In addition, there are some extremely intelligent and somewhat intimidating individuals roaming Bay Street. So again, where do you start?!

My first recommendation is to invest something and "get your feet wet" so to speak. Secondly, as in the world of health, even the most toned individual in the gym started somewhere, thus you should begin to educate yourself. This means, putting in the time to read books, listen to books on tape, attend local financial planning seminars and read the business section. As I stated in my book *Tips From The Top*, become an investor. In other words, it isn't a "sometimes thing", but an actual part of your life. Our planet's greatest investor is Warren Buffet of Omaha, Nebraska. Mr. Buffet has had tremendous success largely due to employing patience when others would not. That is not his only secret, but I believe it to be one of the most important. Thus, patience is my third recommendation. These three steps represent the macro picture. In the immediate future, however, you have made a decision to change your financial life forever, break through the intimidating task of getting started and use the money that you have built as well as future savings optimally.

In order to begin effectively, you must first be of the mind-set that, although you will learn in an almost "spongelike" manner from successful investors, you should aspire to them rather than resent them or allow them to overwhelm you. Also, it is my opinion that when you first begin, it is a time to be slightly selfish. Focus solely on your personal financial position. Once you have begun to build some wealth you may decide to become more philanthropic and more giving with respect to sharing your wealth, as well as your new knowledge, directly with others. Before this however, you should focus on three distinct areas as you start your personal financial plan. These are:

1. What are our short, medium and long-term personal financial goals?

2. Where do we stand today? How much have we built thus far in our lives?

3. What should be our first course(s) of action in the form of investments?

Let's look at these three areas individually and more specifically as they represent a starting point for new, serious investors. Additionally, each represents an opportunity for those people who got serious about wealth building a while ago to review their knowledge.

Your Personal Financial Goals And Objectives

This is, in my opinion, the most important step and the most exciting step in the financial planning process, because it is an opportunity to dream about your financial future. Previously I had mentioned that, as a starting point, you need to be slightly selfish. Often this can be a challenging task because, if you were raised as I was, by hardworking, loving, modest people, the thought of dreaming about your future can seem both frivolous and unrealistic. Start with, "With respect to our future finances, how would we like life to be?" The next question is, "How much money will it take to make those dreams come true?" And finally, "Are we willing to invest this amount and make this commitment to realize our objectives?"

Anyone in business understands goal setting, however whether you are a seasoned business person or a novice investor, what goal we should choose, followed by prioritizing these objectives, is probably the most daunting task. An easy way to tackle this task is to examine a list of potential goals, choose two or three that are extremely motivating and focus your efforts on these until they are achieved and/or another goal that is more important develops in your life. Although it is important to determine if an objective is short, medium or long term, we will discuss this later in the chapter, as our first objective is to compile a list of potential goals. I will give you my generic list and leave some spaces for you to fill in more of your own personal goals. Remember, all goals are possible, and at this point you are "blue skying" and writing down any reasonable goal that comes to mind. Later, you can examine each possible objective to see which ones are the best possible fit for you and your lifestyle.

Generic List Of Objectives

1. Use the generic list of goals and add some of your own "possibilities".

2. Put an X beside the ones that initially interest you.

3. From this X list, scale your goals down to two or three things that you feel are imperative to achieve.

The List

___ Financial independence to our standards, keeping pace with inflation by age _______.

___ To provide money for the ___ partial or ___ full education of our children.

___ To own our home, i.e., be mortgage free and also debt free by age ______.

___ To own a _______________ (type of vehicle) by age _______.

___ To make certain that, in the event of an untimely death, our family is totally cared for financially.

___ I would finally like to be my own boss. I want to own a ___ part time or ___ full time business by age ______.

___ Instead of living pay cheque to pay cheque, I would like a fairly liquid emergency fund of $______.

___ I would like to take a year or two away from my work and do something different (and possibly non-profitable), just for the experience, personal growth and fun.

___ I want excellent knowledge in the area of investment, in order to successfully invest my own portfolio, handle anticipated and inevitable inheritances, as well as to help my children and other family members in building true, long term wealth.

___ I want to own __________ season tickets. (Opera, "Leafs", Ballet, "Oilers", et cetera.)

___ I am interested in returning to school, ___ part time or ___ full time.

___ My investment portfolio must keep pace with inflation forever and this is my main objective.

___ Tax planning is our ongoing priority.

Additional Possible Objectives:
(of your choosing)

—

—

—

—

—

—

—

—

Now that you have gone through the process of scaling down to two or three important financial objectives, time parameters must be drawn to determine short, medium and long term goals. In addition, we need to add in a 4% inflation factor (for our purposes), and figure out approximately, what it will take (in financial terms) to realize your dream. Personally, I consider a short-term goal something that you will try to achieve in 1 to 18 months, such as a comfortable emergency fund or the buying of a new car. A medium-term goal is an objective that can realistically be expected within the next 3 to 5 years. In this case, the objective may be to purchase a new home or to have the savings in place to take a year off work. Anything over 5 years we will call long-term; these include: financial independence or educating your family. There are also "ongoing goals", these feed all the other objectives and may include, saving tax or defeating inflation. What follows is a compound interest table designed to help you calculate your goals and future needs using an arbitrary 4% inflation factor over the next thirty years.

The Compound Growth Table utilizes one dollar of principal: (ie., $1 lump sum invested in advance and compounding annually at 4% in this case)

End of Year	4% Factor	End of Year	4% Factor
1.	1.040	16.	1.873
2.	1.082	17.	1.948
3.	1.125	18.	2.026
4.	1.170	19.	2.107
5.	1.217	20.	2.191
6.	1.265	21.	2.279
7.	1.316	22.	2.370
8.	1.369	23.	2.465
9.	1.423	24.	2.563
10.	1.480	25.	2.666
11.	1.539	26.	2.772
12.	1.601	27.	2.883
13.	1.665	28.	2.999
14.	1.732	29.	3.119
15.	1.801	30.	3.243

Using This Table, Here Is How You Can Get A Very Strong Estimate Of Your Retirement Needs

Example: You are 47 and you want to have $60,000/year in investment income, in today's dollars at age 60.

Calculation is:
\$60,000 x 1.665 = \$99,900/year in 13 years will be required.

Working with a financial advisor, you can then take into account existing RRSPs, pensions and other money to determine your required "lump sum". Now that you have a good idea of where you would like to go in the future, let us examine where you are today. That of course is step 2.

Your Present Financial Position

In this section, we examine what you have accumulated over the last 20, 30, 40 or 50 years! This includes "the good" and "the bad" such as a house, investments, debt and an overall "snapshot" with which you have to work. Using our fitness analogy, it is the equivalent of stripping down, standing in front of the mirror and making some honest, pertinent observations. If you wish, please take the time to fill in the following numbers as they relate to your present financial position:

Total Income

All income (gross and net, monthly and/or yearly):

\$ ________________________________

Expenses

Yearly and/or monthly

Regular savings (RRSPs, etc.) $ ______________

Payments on debt $ ______________

Food and Clothing $ ______________

All shelter expenses $ ______________
(Mtg., rent, utilities, etc.)

All transportation expenses $ ______________
(Insurance, gas, maintenance, etc.)

Recreation and education $ ______________

All other pertinent expenses $ ______________
(miscellaneous)

Your Disposable Income Is:

TOTAL INCOME MINUS
TOTAL EXPENSES = $ ______________

Net Worth * This is the amount that we are trying to build each year.**

Assets

Cash in short term accounts, cash value of life insurance and cash value of your pension plans:

$ ________________________________

Investment values of your home, your RRSPs, your cash accounts including stocks, bonds, GICs, Mutual Funds, etc.:

$ ________________________________

Miscellaneous Assets such as jewelry, cars, boat, etc.:

$ ________________________________

TOTAL OF THESE COMBINED ASSETS =

$ ________________________________

Liabilities

Mortgages owing and loans such as car, business, investment or personal:

$ ________________________________

Credit card balances, outstanding bills, taxes, etc.:

$ ________________________________

Miscellaneous or family debt:

$ ______________________________

TOTAL OF THESE COMBINED LIABILITIES =

$ ______________________________

YOUR NET WORTH IS:

TOTAL ASSETS (minus) TOTAL LIABILITIES =

$ ______________________________

At this juncture we have established what you would like to achieve in the future and where you presently are in life, financially speaking. The last step in financial planning is to establish a course of action. Although we will get more specific with respect to investment strategies as we progress through the book, let me remind you (at the risk of doing some shameless advertising) that my first book has 53 short strategies that can be applied. With respect to taking investment action, again, do your homework!

Some of the questions you may ask prior to embarking on a long-term plan are:

1. What is our expected rate of return?

2. How much risk are we willing to take to achieve that return?

3. Can we handle temporary fluctuations in the financial markets?

4. Are we in this portfolio for the long term?

5. Will these investments meet our objectives? i.e., tax savings, retirement planning, safety, etc.

6. Do we understand the proposed investments?

Congratulations! You have now built an initial record and gained powerful knowledge about yourself today and in the future. This information is powerful because it is straight forward and it recognizes the facts as they relate to you and your family. Admittedly this exercise of facing realities can be difficult. However, nothing is more useful, since knowing the task at hand takes a great deal of the fear out of investing for your future. Moreover, you are moving towards taking some control of your financial life and that always feels terrific! We can now move on to examine specific investment opportunities with the understanding that there is nothing to be intimidated about or fearful of, because we are armed with a financial plan as it pertains to your situation. Now let's plan for tomorrow through investment and by using your new knowledge of who you are today. It is through this knowledge that we can move ahead methodically and confidently.

"Rather than love, than money, than fame, give me truth."

Henry David Thoreau

CHAPTER 4

"CHOOSING YOUR JUNGLE"

In Dr. Stephen Covey's best selling book, *The 7 Habits Of Highly Effective People*, there is a thought provoking section where the author discusses a scenario involving a person "leading" his/her team through a jungle. This "leader" is slashing through thick brush and trees, exerting tremendous energy; and continues to move the team ahead only to find (when the journey is almost complete), that they have worked through "the wrong jungle". This scenario can be effectively applied to one's financial choices. Indeed, if you have been trying to build long-term wealth using GICs and Canada Savings Bonds or making uneducated (and not necessarily the right), decisions when choosing your mutual funds, then you may be slashing your way through the "wrong jungle". Think about it: you have been saving money, and thus you deserve to succeed! However, at the pace you are headed, you will find that (with inflation) you cannot possibly achieve your goals. Certainly none of us ever chooses to be wrong. However, in the wrong type of investment or with the wrong money manager many of us are "spinning our wheels". Considering that the first Boomers have turned fifty years old in 1996, you cannot afford the luxury of choosing "the wrong jungle".

Uninformed investing, then, is not good enough. You must instead invest properly, have an understanding of how each investment works, be aware of what risks and rewards are associated with it; and examine the past performance as well as conservative estimates, with respect to the future growth of an investment. The type of investments you choose will depend on the level of risk you are willing to take, your time frame for investment and your knowledge, as well as that of your advisor. It is obviously key to understand the generics of each investment type, whether it is too passive or too aggressive in nature, so that you can make educated decisions and work towards your goals with confidence. Below are a few descriptions of several different investments.

These investments will be described briefly. For a more comprehensive description of how these can be applied to your personal situation, contact your advisor and ask him or her to meet with you.

Fixed Income Products (GICS, Term Deposits And Bonds).

These are referred to as fixed income products because we know the rate of return when we purchase the investment. For example, if you purchase a 5 year GIC at 6.75% compounding annually, then you have entered into an agreement to allow an institution to hold your money for five years. In exchange for that right, the institution pays you 6.75% every year and compounds that new amount with interest in each of the five years. The key is that you will not receive any more or less for your investment than 6.75% per year for the five year period.

The major difference between Term Deposits and GICs is the period of time over which the investment is "tied up". In the case of a term deposit, you usually "lock money up" for 30, 60 or 90 days at a time and as money comes due you can take it out to spend, position it into a new investment type or just renew it into another Term Deposit. This investment has a relatively low rate of return over the long term, is interest bearing and thus, fully taxable outside of an RRSP. As a result, it is best suited for short term goals such as paying down an upcoming debt or for a child's education in the fall, etc. As a long term investment towards retirement, it is not the best option as you will have major difficulty keeping pace with rising costs due to inflation. GICs have the same basic properties as do Term Deposits but with a 1 to 5 year term in relation to "locking up your money". These investments are for conservative investors or individuals so wealthy that rates of return and tax considerations do not matter to them; they want safety. These investments are covered by $60,000 of deposit insurance, however, I personally would not be afraid to invest above this amount if the institution is solid, such as one of Canada's major Chartered banks. The main thing is that if you are concerned, ask about your protection.

Another interesting product that is offered by insurance companies is the "RRIF to 90". Registered Retirement Income Funds are of course, how we Boomers will receive income from all of these RRSPs we are building over the next many years. They are very similar to GICs, the difference being the period of time over which the investment return is fixed. If, for example, rates are fairly high, you might be satisfied receiving 10% per year in your RRIF; guaranteed for say, 30 or 35 years. My main point of caution with respect to these longer terms, however, is be pretty darn certain that the company will be around tomorrow. Thirty years is a long time to commit to an insurance company you do not know intimately. Boomers do not yet have to worry about the decision of locking in retirement income payments quite yet. Instead, the challenge is to build up enough money towards retirement so that they won't have those worries with respect to retirement income.

Another excellent fixed income product that allows one to use a combination of guarantees and speculation with respect to interest rates, are bonds. Bonds are an excellent investment from a standpoint of flexibility and potential opportunity. These investments are issued as municipal, provincial, federal and corporate bonds. Each bond has a fixed rate of return attached to it and, as is the case with a GIC, if you hold a bond until maturity, you will know the rate of return in advance. Bonds have a major advantage over GICs, however, as they offer liquidity as well as the possibility of capital gains. Bonds are "traded" daily on the market with the price being determined by the safety of the bond and more importantly, by interest rates. If interest rates are rising, the value of your bond will drop; however, if rates are going down, your bond's value will rise, giving you the opportunity to sell it out and thus create a capital gain. Bonds have 1 to 30 year terms. Thus, for a bond speculator it is important to note that the longer the term, the more volatile a bond value will be with respect to the potential gain or loss. Thus, if a bond investor feels strongly that rates are heading down, he/she may purchase a 30 year bond with the intention of selling it for a capital gain in the near future. A smaller bet on lower interest rates, but offering the same intention of procuring a capital gain, would be to purchase a 10 year bond (or even a 3 year bond) to limit the exposure in your portfolio in case rates do not react as you think they may. Regardless, even if all you do is hold the bond until maturity and receive the guaranteed rate, bonds can be a fabulous investment. Accordingly, to a certain degree they can usually fit nicely into almost any portfolio.

For the non-speculator who is conservative and also smart enough not to try to outguess interest rates, a great way to use GICs and bonds is by using a laddered portfolio. If for example, you are placing money strategically in 1,2,3,4 and 5 year terms and as a result, you have money coming due yearly, you will even-out aberrations in interest rates. In the case of a Bond portfolio, you may wish to choose maturity dates that go beyond five years, but regardless, this strategy is good for Boomers building an RRSP portfolio, as well as for your parents who may need a stable, guaranteed income.

Preferred Shares

There are many different types of preferred shares, so I will not go into specifics. Rather, my purpose here is to give you enough information to work effectively with your broker/advisor; not to necessarily become one! In short, preferred shares are suitable for a fairly conservative investor who is looking for ongoing dividend payments and the possibility of a capital gain. While this investment allows ownership in shares of a company with traditionally less risk than common shares it can, however, realize strong potential returns. Although a Boomer may explore this investment as a portion of his/her portfolio, these shares are very popular among investors who desire income from an investment. Indeed, rather than an interest bearing investment, such as a GIC, (which outside an RRSP is fully taxable), "preferreds" garner tax preferred treatment through the dividend tax credit.

Common Shares

Many of the world's truly great investors share a common philosophy with respect to common shares. That is, rather than going out and "buying a stock", they are "buying a company". What this means for you is that if, for example, you purchase even 100 shares of General Motors you should focus on the fact that you are going into the automobile industry. Thus the question then becomes, should you? Also, ask yourself if you want to be in business with GM? Regardless of which company's shares you purchase, you should consider, is management sound? What is its track record and future prospects? Finally, do I understand the business? After all, how can you go into a business that neither you nor your financial advisor even remotely understand? The "Warren Buffet way" has been dissected and discussed at length in financial circles over the past few years. The reason for this interest in Mr. Buffet's philosophy is quite simple - nothing has worked better over the long term. Mr. Buffet's philosophy is to buy "value" companies such as Coca-Cola, Walt Disney and The Washington Post, among others, and hold them for the long term. This method has proven itself to be outstanding as these companies do consistently increase in value and are safe investments. Moreover, the "buy and hold" strategy is efficient from a standpoint of both tax deferral as well as in saving the cost of unnecessary trades and commissions. This, however, is only one way of purchasing shares.

Another method, although more volatile, is to speculate on smaller, less established companies for the potential of greater gains. Remember, Microsoft was once small, as was Alcan Aluminum, Dofasco, Nova Corp. and Shell. If you are working with a competent advisor who has excellent research and a handle on how a business operates the risk can be "cut back" considerably. My recommendation is to purchase the smaller capital businesses in conjunction with less volatile investments and always spread the risk through diversification. The main point is that maybe you should not ignore smaller companies completely. Indeed, a forty-five year old Boomer may have only fifteen or twenty years to build for retirement and thus he or she needs an average of twelve to fifteen percent annually. Thus, most Boomers are young enough to explore all their investment options fully and, as is usually the case for Boomers, are quite often successful in their endeavors.

Mutual Funds

Mutual funds invest in many different areas such as Canadian and International equities, bonds, mortgages, T-bills, precious metals, small to mid-size companies and an array of other specialties in the investment arena. Mutual funds provide instant diversification and are an outstanding investment for any person, particularly a Baby Boomer who wants strong returns and most of all, hassle-free, inexpensive, professional management. With all of these positives, are there any potential pitfalls? In a word, definitely. First, these are long-term investments; five years or better as a buy and hold strategy. Also, funds fluctuate, meaning these are not GICs, so you must be prepared for some "ups and downs" and this again lends itself to trusting the portfolio manager. When evaluating a fund manager or fund family, do not ignore new players in the game, but that said, as a rule of thumb "past performance means everything". For example: Mr. Rolex is a successful Boomer with his own business and in the vernacular, he has "finally made it"! He wants to show the world! Mr. Rolex withdraws $110,000 from his corporate account and heads down to the local Mercedes dealership where he purchases his dream car. First stop, home to his spouse and children. Next stop, his parents house to make them proud. Third stop, his ex-girlfriend's house (the one who dumped him in college for the most popular guy on campus who is now on welfare). Indeed, life is just a bowl of cherries! Now, since I am his financial advisor, Mr. Rolex swings by my office to take me out for a spin. Ten minutes into our drive the engine seizes. The car cannot be fixed and he has purchased "a lemon". I certainly believe the first part of our scenario may come true. The second part, however, about the engine seizing, would be nearly impossible in the case of a new "Benz" because over the years, Mercedes has built a reputation based on making outstanding cars and their engineers will not go into work tomorrow and "forget how".

Similarly, in the area of mutual funds, professional managers such as Trimark, Templeton, Fidelity, A.I.C., A.G.F. and Mackenzie, to name a few, have been building wealth for people just like you for a long time now. They each own a philosophy that has proven itself in good markets and bad. Over the long-term, all have produced outstanding results for clients. The danger though, is that all money managers are not created equal. At the time of this writing, I am examining two seemingly similar Canadian equity funds. One is well diversified, does take long term security into account and has averaged over 20% per year for the past five years. The other, a major bank's version of the same fund has averaged 4.5% per year over the same five year period. The answer then to negotiating your way through over 1,000 mutual funds, is to procure professional and "unbiased" help and research. While there are some outstanding "no load" funds from which to choose, remember, you are also subject for the most part to "no advice". For a sophisticated investor, this is certainly an option. For busy people who want help and do not want to devote 60% of their time to analyzing investments, "load" funds with outstanding advice are appropriate. Also, "no load" does not mean "free", as there is still a management fee and it is usually very similar to that of "load" funds.

The bottom line is this: Mutual Funds are an increasingly popular investment, but it is important to do some homework and have your advisor show you his or her homework. Again, "past performance means everything" as does information with respect to changes in the fund's investment strategy, as well as in their key personnel.

Commodities And Options

Commodities and options are certainly more volatile and sophisticated investments. For the wealthy Baby Boomer who understands the markets and wishes to attempt to enhance returns with the help of an outstanding "specialist" in these areas; these can fit well into a portfolio. You can access these investments and these "specialists" at most major investment firms, as well as through some recent Mutual Fund offerings. Although, I have said these vehicles are usually associated with "high rolling risk takers", they may also be used as a very conservative strategy. For example, as an investor you may use options to take advantage of a stock you feel may rise and yet have the advantage of a more limited and known risk at the outset. Options can also be used to firm up a maximum price that one will pay for a stock at a later date or to lock in today's price. Although these vehicles can also be put in place to protect your investments from an erratic drop in the price of an individual stock, they are not to be entered into without a firm understanding and a solid, open relationship with a broker who specializes in these areas. If you would like to "get your feet wet" and learn as you go, a Managed Futures Mutual Fund may get you started. Then, as you become more comfortable, you may wish to progress to a more specialized position. Investing in areas such as grains, metals, financial futures, soybeans, cocoa and coffee (to name a few), may not be for everyone. However, gaining an understanding of this area can be invaluable inside your portfolio.

Regardless Of Your Investment Mix, Strong Rates Of Return Are Imperative

Relationships with trustworthy, competent professionals are very important. This, however, must be coupled with strong, long-term rates of return for the Boomer. Many of you have no doubt heard of "The Rule of 72". In short, for those who have not, this easy calculation states that if you take your average compound annual rate of return, and divide it into 72, this is the amount of time that it will take for your lump sum to double.

Thus, for example, Joe, age 37 is conservative, has not done his homework but has saved $25,000 in an RRSP that will achieve 8% per year compound growth. He is "satisfied" with this. His twin sister, Jane is also fairly conservative, but has done her homework and is an astute investor. She also has $25,000 in an RRSP and will be able to achieve 12% per year compound growth over the long term. This is, of course, hypothetical; but lets look at the difference that a well planned portfolio and thus an additional 4% return would make over time.

Joe		**Jane**	
Age 37	$ 25,000	Age 37	$ 25,000
72 ÷ 8% per year = 9 years		72 ÷ 12% per year = 6 years	
Age 46	$ 50,000	Age 43	$ 50,000
		Age 49	$100,000
Age 55	$100,000	Age 55	$200,000
		Age 61	$400,000
Age 64	$200,000	Age 64	$562,000

In Summary

The creed of the Boomer in 1996 is one of focus and goal setting. These skills are a couple of the components that have made so many Boomers successful as business people, technologists, teachers, doctors and as entrepreneurs. It is these skills that will further propel Boomers into a successful retirement and create opportunities as investors. We have looked briefly at several different investment avenues that are available to us as we build personal wealth, however, the idea of personal wealth is different to each individual investor. To one person, it is to be out of debt, educate two children and have a $100,000 RRSP, plus a company pension. A second person may want to travel the world, create philanthropic opportunities for others and feels that a portfolio worth $50,000,000 is needed to live as she or he wishes.

Regardless of how you envision "wealth", it is key that you understand the opportunities that will create your financial future. Equally important are the aforementioned skills of focus and goal setting so that you may determine which investment vehicles will fit your personal style and which has the best probability to act as a catalyst in moving you toward your goals. Finally, incorporate a mix of investments that will provide safety, yet strong, long-term results.

My advice is simple, learn about the many investment opportunities available, focus on the products you understand the best; and then work with a financial professional in order to maximize your effectiveness and your returns as an investor. As you do this, consistently look to the long term and try to fight off the influence of media and the negative people who surround you and who do not understand your personal goals and situation. If it were easy, everyone would build wealth. Clearly the difference between those investors who achieve and those who fail lies in both intelligent decisions and "stick-to-itiveness". The key for the Boomer is to draw on the two skills that have become synonymous with our generation: focus on your immediate investment decisions and keep your eyes on the long term objective. It is through this approach that we will achieve one victory at a time as we, as a generation, build long-term wealth. Paupers do not have to concern themselves with investment decisions and we have learned not to depend on our government, our employer or our rich aunt to retire as we wish. Thus the choice for the Boomer is obvious, take control financially or pay the price of not putting in the effort or the investment. It is up to each of us, individually. We must commit to invest and choose "the right jungle".

"There are a million excuses for not paying the price. If only I was given a particular opportunity or if only the coach, teacher or boss liked me better, I could have accomplished this or that. Nothing but excuses."

Michael Jordan.

CHAPTER 5

START WITH A LITTLE, END UP WITH A LOT!

In the late sixties and early seventies the battle for my allowance and (if you will permit me to assume) the allowance of many of you, raged. In the neighbourhood where I grew up, the scene was always the same. It was usually ninety degrees on a clear summer day and there were about ten or twelve kids playing baseball or football in the park, or even road hockey on the street. Usually around two in the afternoon each day it happened: That familiar bell rang and then...pandemonium! Was it Dickey Dee on his bike or The Good Humour Man in his little white truck? (Or was it the knife sharpener torturing us again while, like Pavlovian dogs, our little mouths watered at the sound of any bell?) Were they sold out of "Fudgecicles" and "Ice Cream Sandwiches" by this time of day? How much time did I have to get my money and get back to him? If the driver was in a generous mood, he would wait. If he was "power tripping" that day it was my belief that he would intentionally speed away as I bound out of the house having taken a few extra minutes to scrape together my money. The comedian, Eddie Murphy, has a skit about this everyday occurrence and the anxiety that each of us felt as we tried to complete this transaction. Unlike Mr. Murphy, our neighbourhood purchased ice cream without a whole bunch of four letter words. Seriously though, none of the kids on our street received money from their parents for ice cream every day and my house was no exception. My parents were good to my brothers and me. Although we certainly did our part to keep Dickie Dee and Good Humour profitable, at times my mother or father would say, "If I had the money handy I would give it to you. Unfortunately, I just do not have it today." Ironically, I have often heard a very similar argument concerning a much more important subject than ice cream, that is, with respect to starting to build an investment portfolio for retirement.

"We're just getting by and making ends meet, how could we ever invest?" My solution to this dilemma is simple, keep buying your children ice cream, but give it up yourselves and use the money to invest in an RRSP until your retirement. As I stated in *Tips From The Top*, to leverage this opportunity, it is best to also reinvest your tax savings and we will look at this later. In the meantime, the last time I checked, an ice cream bar or cone was at least $1.65 at the corner store. What this means is that if you are a two-parent household this gives you $3.30 per day to invest. Over the course of a full year, you would have $1,204.50 invested into an RRSP. Furthermore, assuming (for example) you are forty years old and that you are in a forty percent tax bracket, you could invest tax savings of $481.80 per year in addition to your original investment until retirement at say, age sixty-five.

Here is the math:

Assuming you are going to use what you learn in this book, you should be able to average a long-term investment return on growth type investments of 12% or better, overall. I will also assume that you are reinvesting all dividends and that your tax refund comes to you in cash. It is important to note that you could reinvest your refund in an RRSP to enhance your yearly tax savings, but for our purposes, because some investors want non-registered securities, our numbers will not reflect a better tax position or possible gains owing on non-registered accounts. Instead, we will look at raw numbers.

$1,204.50/year ($100.38/month or two ice cream bars per day) @ 12% growth for 25 years = $179,872.80.

$481.80 (tax savings reinvested) @ 12% compound growth as well for 25 years = $71,949.12

YOUR GRAND TOTAL = $251,821.92.

In order to keep pace with inflation, check the price of an ice cream bar every few months and raise your monthly investment accordingly. Also, as you get raises in your income, as the mortgage is retired, as your car payment or credit card payment diminishes, increase your investment accordingly. Recently, I was asked on a Montreal radio station what the "cut off date" was for people who want to build money for retirement? For Baby Boomers, there really is no "cut-off date" although considering that the oldest Boomers are now fifty years of age, time is of the essence. Regardless, my answer to this question is that it is all dependent on each person's personal commitment to themselves. Just as saving $100/month beginning at age forty can produce a quarter of a million dollars at sixty-five, $500/month ($6,000/year) under this same structure with your tax refund re-invested will give you approximately $1.25 million! (assuming 12% compound returns as an average over twenty-five years.)

Your advisor can do the math for you based on your age and what you can afford. My point, however, is that almost anyone can actually afford to get started with an investment portfolio and, the fact is, you must. Employers, our government and even our fellow citizens will have very little sympathy for people in the future who worked for thirty or forty years and have nothing to show for it. Instead, it is my opinion that our dollars should (and ultimately will) be reserved for the unfortunate group who would have worked, and would have gladly saved, but for one reason or another, could not; rather than the individual or couple who blew all of their extra money on ice cream. Of course, I am being factitious and somewhat harsh, however, please believe that my heart is in the right place: I am genuinely concerned.

So you are ready to save $3.30 per day (or more) and get started on the road to long-term wealth. With that commitment, we can begin to examine some popular options with respect to methods of actually getting your money invested. Two popular methods of forced savings are "Dollar Cost Averaging" and "Leveraging" through an investment loan. The first method of investing we will examine, dollar cost averaging, is the more conservative of the two options and is extremely effective as a means of building a fortune inside your RRSP. Next we will look at leveraging, named for its ability to accentuate gains and losses particularly over the short-term. This is a more aggressive approach to investing than dollar averaging and can be extremely effective, if used properly as a long-term strategy. Moreover, it can even create a tax write-off for those people who have little or no room to contribute inside an RRSP. These two methods can work separately or together to form a long-term wealth building plan that can be extremely formidable as you attack the seemingly monumental task of retirement planning.

Dollar Cost Averaging

A good friend of mine is a chess fanatic. He will play anywhere, anytime and in most cases, he will win. A terrific invention that came out a few years back is a computerized chess game that allows a person to always have an intelligent and willing opponent: a battle for supremacy pitting humankind against the microchip. Recently, I caught my friend playing chess on his machine, but the computer was turned off and he was using physical chess pieces. I said, "Excuse me Jim, but why are you taking both sides of the table and playing against yourself?" Jim replied, "Because no matter what, I will eventually win!" Imagine if you could invest this way! If this were possible, you could win in bull or bear markets, you would take advantage of falling prices and build equity as the market increased in value. Indeed, you could invest in fairly aggressive portfolios, but have the advantage of taking a passive approach. Thus the investment "glass", so to speak, would always seem half-full as opposed to often seeming half-empty as would be the case in volatile markets. In other words, no matter what, you would eventually win. This, in a nutshell, is dollar cost averaging.

Simply put, dollar cost averaging is the practice of investing identical amounts of money each month for an extended period of time into a single investment or an array of investments regardless of fluctuations in the market at large or in the investments in which you are participating. The long-term result is threefold, first, because the price of your investment will fluctuate over time, you are not locked-in to any one purchase price. Instead, you are buying in at many prices and this will give you an "average" price with respect to each investment. In other words, if I purchase $12,000 worth of XYZ at $6 per share, I am hoping for a significant rise in the shares of XYZ over time, (assuming this is not a short term speculative purchase). Still, a different option is to invest $1,000 per month into XYZ over the course of one year. In this case each individual $1,000 will buy shares at a different price, producing an average share price that is hopefully in my favour. Irrespective of this, dollar cost averaging is clearly a much more tentative approach to buying XYZ.

The second benefit, and in my opinion the greatest benefit of dollar cost averaging, is the long term advantage of winning on both ends with respect to market fluctuations. This can only be the case, however, providing you are committed to the long-term and if you are purchasing a solid investment that will fluctuate, but will not die. In the latter case, all you have achieved is putting a great deal of money (on a monthly basis) into a declining investment that is eventually worth nothing. Using a more reasonable scenario, when a specific investment, or the markets in general, are declining, you are buying more shares to capitalize on down markets thus positioning yourself to win when the markets go up again. An example is as follows:

You decide to invest $250/month into the Baby Boomers Value and Growth Fund (especially when you find out that it has a five year average return of 31.2%). Keeping in mind that you are committed to this in good times and bad, for richer and poorer and in sickness as well as health; here is what your investment may look like:

Month
1: $250 invested at $6.00/unit=You buy 41.66 units.
2: $250 invested at $6.23/unit=You buy 40.13 units.
3: $250 invested at $6.84/unit=You buy 36.55 units.
4: $250 invested at $7.54/unit=You buy 33.16 units.
****Note: Your shares are going up very nicely in value, however, you are purchasing fewer units each month.

Month
5: $250 invested at $8.15/unit=You buy 30.67 units.
6: $250 invested at $7.16/unit=You buy 34.92 units.
7: $250 invested at $6.91/unit=You buy 36.18 units.
8: $250 invested at $5.32/unit=You buy 46.99 units.
9: $250 invested at $4.13/unit=You buy 60.53 units.
10: $250 invested at $4.11/unit=You buy 60.83 units.
11: $250 invested at $3.79/unit=You buy 65.96 units.
12: $250 invested at $5.85/unit=You buy 42.74 units.

After only one year and an extremely volatile year for your Baby Boomers Fund, here are some interesting results:

If you had invested the full $3,000 at the beginning of the year when units were $6, your investment would be worth $2,925 today. In other words, you purchased 500 units that are now worth $5.85/unit.

*** Thus your one year return is a negative 2.5%.

You are a long term investor and, therefore, you do not worry. Although dollar cost averaging will lose some significant advantage in rising, "bullish" markets, it will be wise in uncertain conditions, such as the one illustrated below:

Here is your position after a year:

$3,000 invested in even $250/month increments.

You own 530.32 units at an average $5.85/unit.

Your portfolio, although the market is down from where you began, actually gained 3.4%.

This represents a difference of 5.9% in the two strategies, again only examining the short term.

On your $3,000 investment, this 5.9% only equates to a difference of $177. However, what if you are contemplating an investment of $3,000,000 but are concerned about market conditions. In our scenario, after one year using dollar cost averaging and investing $250,000/month, you would be ahead the same 5.9% or $177,000. Thus, for a slightly nervous investor this can be a strategy that will allow peace of mind. Moreover, if the market begins to take off, you always have the option of moving out of your monthly investment plan and moving all of your investment into the markets immediately.

I had mentioned a third benefit of dollar cost averaging and the clue to this is in our illustration. Not every Boomer is a high income earner, not all save well, and many do not have access to a large sum of money but, ironically, many of you eventually want a large retirement portfolio. Thus, the third advantage of dollar cost averaging is that you can invest regular, small amounts (such as $250/month) into an investment and get yourself started. This is commonly used in the area of Mutual Fund investment and is taken right out of your bank account electronically every month for the purchase of your investment. In the end, it is a great way to buy your RRSP and alleviates the problem of coming up with that needed lump sum just after Christmas.

Leveraging

Today, you have to perform two hypothetical transactions at the bank. First, you are purchasing an RRSP. Your contribution limit is $10,000 so you put the money into an RRSP/GIC for 5 years at a rate of 6.25%. Next, it is over to the loans department to chat about your husband's new minivan. You explain that the cost of the new van is $26,500 and that you are willing to put down $16,500. You would, however, like a $10,000 loan to cover the remaining cost with the monthly payments to be "as low as possible". The loans officer suggests, "spreading the payments over five years." You then ask, "What's the rate on my $10,000 loan?" He replies, "It's going to be 9.5%". In essence, you have just borrowed back your own money at a cost of 3.25% per year, every year for five years. This course of action is necessary because you need the RRSP to save you from the "tax man" and your spouse needs the minivan immediately, but what a raw deal! You give the bank your money and they invest it in the form of a loan and, in this case, make a "spread" of 3.25%. It is no wonder that they have the tallest buildings on Bay Street. These people are smart and it seems so simple! In that case, why don't you do it?

The concept of leveraging involves borrowing money from a bank at a lower rate than what your long-term investment will produce over a period of time such as five years or more. To tip the scales even further in your favour, the interest portion of the loan is tax deductible, thus bringing your "break-even point" down to an even lower level. For example, you are in a fifty percent tax bracket and you own your home outright. In addition, your cash flow is excellent and because of a strong pension at work, you are only allowed to invest $2,300 per year in an RRSP. In this case you may go to a bank or a trust company and take out a home equity line of credit using your home as collateral, thus securing an excellent rate on your loan. For our example, let's assume that your home is worth $300,000 and you take a loan of $50,000. Let us further suppose that your preferred rate is 7.5% and you are required to pay the institution "interest only" on the loan. In the end, you are getting some of the equity "out of your home" in a fairly conservative fashion and considering your 50% tax bracket, one half of your loan payment will be returned to you as a tax refund. In this example, your "break-even point" is only 3.75% or 7.5% divided by two. Surely a well thought-out, long-term portfolio can work well in this situation. So, why isn't everyone flocking to their local bank branch?

First, you must take a very long-term view of these investments. Stated plainly, in temporary down markets, your statements can look ugly and in these cases, not only are you losing money in your portfolio, but you are paying the bank monthly for that privilege. For a Boomer who is stressed out about retirement, this position, albeit temporary, can appear catastrophic. As a financial advisor, I recommend you approach this strategy gingerly with respect to both the amount of debt you will take on initially, as well as with respect to the position you are willing to take regarding your monthly payment to the bank. Finally, it is common for these investment loans to be on a fluctuating rate scale. As a result, your "comfortable monthly payment" to the bank could go up by thirty or forty percent if interest rates rise unexpectedly. It is important, therefore, to leave yourself some breathing space.

The investment loan can be extremely effective, particularly for those Baby Boomers who wish to enhance their position and maximize their investments outside their RRSP. To take full advantage of it, however, you should be in a high tax bracket, have no debt, have a very strong cash flow, an excellent understanding of the concept itself (as well as an understanding of the tax implications including capital gains and C.N.I.L rules), but most of all, work with an excellent advisor who is consulting you in your best interest. One of the reasons why leveraging has gotten a bad rap in the past is due to commission driven "salespeople" (not financial advisors). Often these "salespersons" have placed people into these programs who have heavy debt, cannot afford the payments, do not understand the inherent short term risks; and are not even fully utilizing the room inside their RRSP. In the end, investment loans are a tremendous avenue for well heeled Boomers as a means of building retirement money outside an RRSP, but nonetheless, you must work to understand this strategy prior to getting started.

The Boomers' Secret Weapon: Compound Interest

By now, you have all seen a chart describing the wonders of compound interest. If you were as afraid as I had described in Chapter 2, these encouraging numbers, backed by a personal commitment to yourself, will abate your fears. Let us take an example. You are 45 years old and you want $1,000,000 before tax by age 60 on which to retire and you wish to keep pace with inflation. Your portfolio is worth $45,000 but you now own a $350,000 home and can afford a $10,000 per year RRSP and a $35,000 investment loan, very comfortably. You are in a 50% tax bracket so you can utilize the tax benefits and reinvest the yearly refund. So, why will compound interest be your "secret weapon" over the next fifteen years?

First, let us look at what you will invest over that period of time: $45,000 is already invested, $150,000 will go into your RRSP over the next 15 years and we will assume it will take an average of $5,000 per year to manage your investment loan for an overall investment of $75,000. Once again, assuming a 12% average compound rate of return on your portfolio, here are the figures:

Overall fifteen year total investment equals $270,000. ($45,000 + $150,000 + $75,000).

$45,000 @ 12% for 15 years = $246,330

$10,000/yr. @ 12% for 15 years = $417,530

$35,000 investment @ 12% for 15 years =
$191,590 - $35,000 loan = $156,590

Add to this tax refunds of approximately $7,500/year for fifteen years that will have resulted from the write-offs of a $10,000 RRSP; and from paying approximately $5,000/year for the investment loan. You decide to take a holiday with $2,500 of this refund every year and you reinvest the remaining $5,000 back into your portfolio. Again, without the aid of compounding, you have invested only $75,000, but:

Using our assumed 12% annual compounding rate, $5,000/year @ 12% for 15 years = $208,765

Adjusted total invested since you began this strategy at age 45 (including your previously saved $45,000, $150,000, $75,000 as well as $75,000 of "government assistance") equals $345,000.

YOUR RETIREMENT PORTFOLIO TOTAL (BEFORE TAX) = $1,029,215! ! !

So, fear not! Instead, utilize your assets, your cash flow, your tax position and your knowledge, as well as the knowledge of a great advisor and his or her firm. In the end, you can create a solid portfolio in a fairly short period of time using the conservative method of dollar cost averaging, and an aggressive strategy of leveraging (only if you are in the proper position and have a full understanding) and allow compound interest to do the rest! The key is to stay abreast of new developments in the markets and stick with the plan. Above all, do not let people talk you into investments that you cannot understand and that cannot be explained in very easy terms to you as the investor. It is imperative that you feel comfortable with a strategy so that it stands the test of volatile markets. Only then will you be comfortable enough to allow your investments the time to grow and mature into a powerful portfolio.

"Never invest in any idea you can't illustrate with a crayon".

Peter Lynch, from his book; *Beating the Street.*

CHAPTER 6

KEEPING YOUR SHARE

"Greed is good!" bellowed Michael Douglas in his role as Gordon Gecko in the Oliver Stone movie "Wall Street". Although many Boomers embraced this philosophy in the eighties, I believe that now, a few years older, we have mellowed considerably. In fact, a business person who would openly state that greed is his or her motivation in 1997 would look ridiculous. Imagine a Canadian chartered bank president posting a one billion dollar profit at their annual meeting and proclaiming that "Greed is Good!" Certainly, Boomers still want the good things in life, but now we want it in balance. Boomers want wealth but will forego "super-wealth" for more family time. Moreover, we want a fit and healthy lifestyle, but we do not necessarily want to give up items such as imported beer, good wine, red meat, cigars, or my personal favourite, Starbuck's coffee. Ninety-hour work weeks (if they still exist) are concealed due to embarrassment. They have instead been replaced with a fifty-hour work week, acute time management and more time on the golf course and ski slopes. If Oliver Stone creates a movie in a few years depicting the nineties-style Boomer business person, it should consist of a team of men and women, some working out of their homes, dedicated to family and leisure activities, with the moniker, "Balance is Good!" So, as I ponder a chapter on "Keeping Your Share", I, as a financial advisor, contemplate the importance of saving tax, not being overcharged for goods and services and making certain that as an investor, you are receiving the growth you deserve on your investment. However, I do not believe that we need to be as anxious about it as we have been in the past. Instead, let us take a calm look at how to keep your share as it pertains to tax, commissions on investments and other items; but with the understanding that quality costs money. To be sure, "quality" has a vast scope, it includes the quality of our roads, our children's education, our healthcare, all investment advice and most other aspects of our lives.

In *Tips From The Top*, we dedicated an entire section to saving income tax and reducing debt, two important areas in keeping your share. There are many great strategies with respect to tax reduction and for very specific ideas regarding your personal position, please speak to your financial advisor. In general, the concepts of saving tax, reducing debt and searching for value in your investments, as well as the nature of your relationship with a financial advisor and his or her firm, are paramount to long term success. So let's take a look at these areas in the context of creating a strong portfolio designed to achieve excellent results. Ultimately, this portfolio should allow you to feel good about how you are investing with respect to keeping your share of the profits that you, as an investor, certainly deserve.

One obvious way of keeping your share is by giving the government less. People all over the country curse and berate our government as they file their tax returns yearly and vow to pay less tax the following year. Still, some use it as a badge of honour at cocktail parties. Recently, a gentleman whom I barely knew (and who did not realize what I did for a living) exclaimed to my wife and me at a social engagement, "damn government, I paid $163,000 in income tax last year!"

He even managed to act angry although his real message was clearly, "I'm wealthy and I want you to know it". As for you people who actually do not like paying undue income tax, here are some fundamental ideas to work on with your financial advisor.

To begin with, in Canada we have a great opportunity for deferring income tax, the Registered Retirement Savings Plan. Consequently, each individual should put away as much money as they possibly can into this vehicle until they reach the age of sixty-nine. Not only are RRSPs a fantastic deal from a standpoint of tax deferral, they also often contribute to a tax refund each year that you can reinvest towards building wealth. Each year the federal government makes us aware of the amount we are allowed to put into RRSPs. For you Boomers who have not made the most of your contribution limits in the past, but are now coming into money through either debt reduction or inheritance, your goal should be to invest as much as you can, as quickly as you can, in your RRSP. For example, some of you may have a contribution limit, carried forward from years past, of $34,000. Moreover, you may have just received an inheritance of $78,000. If you were a high income earner and you had this type of contribution room then you would receive approximately one-half of the $34,000 back as a refund. This would give you an additional $17,000 to reinvest almost immediately, along with the remaining inheritance. My advice, however, is to work with a tax professional so as to invest your maximum effectively and to avoid alternate minimum tax.

As we have discussed in the previous chapter, borrowing money to invest or "leveraging", creates a tax write-off since the interest portion of an investment loan is tax deductible as a carrying charge. A word of caution, in the case of an investment loan with which you entered into a long term investment in the hope of a long-term tax write-off; be aware that you have no control over how our government will treat this type of investment over an extended period of time. Thus, with respect to leveraging, the main focus should be long-term growth through quality investing, rather than simply a long term tax strategy that can be altered or even eliminated during the next Federal budget. Another non-registered investment that you may find interesting from a standpoint of tax savings and potential growth, is the Mutual Fund Limited Partnership.

The Mutual Fund L.P. is a very popular investment, particularly for a client who is a high income earning Baby Boomer in need of strong write-offs.

The main problem, however, is the popularity of this investment and thus the difficulty of all financial advisors in procuring enough of an offering to satisfy his or her client base. In essence, what you are purchasing is a form of a partnership with a fund company and even some participation in their management fee. These partnerships are arbitrarily brought out by fund companies in order to fund commissions to brokers and financial planners. Moreover, they provide the potential for strong growth, income from the investment and the ability to write-off the entire investment (one-third at a time) for the first three years. The investment is usually a fifteen year obligation. However, as in the case of most investments, some aftermarket does exist. The real key is that you should ultimately become "partners" with a mutual fund company that is strong, has good, positive cash flow rather than redemptions and excellent management. If you can achieve this you will, once again, keep more of your share.

Presently, billions of dollars sit in non-registered, fixed income products in Canada. These include GICs, Canada Savings Bonds, Term Deposits and Corporate, Municipal, Provincial and Federal Bonds. Each of these is interest bearing and the interest earned is one hundred percent taxable. It is very important to note, however, that Corporate, Municipal, Provincial and Federal bonds can be sold (quite easily) in the aftermarket to create a capital gain. This capital gain is a tax advantage in that only seventy-five percent of the gain is taxable. Thus, for efficient investing from a tax standpoint, investments that produce capital gains such as the aforementioned bonds, stocks, mutual funds, etc., are advisable. Dividends from mutual funds, as well as dividends paid from profits in relation to other investments, qualify for the dividend tax credit and will assist you in your quest to give less to the government. All of the strategies mentioned thus far, are fairly rudimentary forms of tax planning and can be easily implemented after discussions with your financial advisor. If we are looking for a moral to this particular story it is that you need not be a "rocket scientist" to be efficient from a tax standpoint. You must, however, make a slight paradigm shift away from GICs. Without a doubt these new opportunities create more volatility in a portfolio. As Boomers, though, we are still young and can thus handle it, since the trade-off offers the potential for outstanding long term results, as well as the chance to hold on to more of our tax dollars each and every year.

Switching gears slightly, let us consider another form of keeping your share, debt reduction. Reducing your debt reduces interest payments and without those payments your monthly income belongs to you, thus, giving you the opportunity to expedite your creation of wealth. Many Boomers are either paying off a mortgage, some may have already done so, but more often than not, debt and monthly payments that are not tax deductible continue to exist. For those of you who have not paid off your debt to your own satisfaction, it is here that you should focus your efforts. There is no way around it, paying off debt requires sacrifice and discipline. In the case of a mortgage, your goal may be to bring the amortization down from ten years to five years of payments. In the beginning, this is a very non-gratifying exercise as you seem to be barely "making a dent" for the first year or so, but in the long run it is worth it. Discipline is necessary to keep you focused on the goal of being debt free, having no more monthly payments, freeing up money to invest and ultimately keeping more of your share. What then, is the benefit of paying off a ten year debt in five years that would normally require, for example, $1,000 per month? Apart from the interest you have denied your local banker, the less obvious benefit is freeing up $1,000 per month for the next five years. If we achieved average compound growth on your portfolio of 12%, you would have no debt, plus $85,380, before tax, in ten years! All of this just by paying off your commitment 5 years earlier and investing your monthly payments.

In terms of how to create the discipline to sacrifice and pay off debt early my recommendation, as old fashioned and as simple as it is, would be to think of it as a bill. This way, you will put extra away towards your debt each and every month. In addition, earmark things like company bonuses, part of an inheritance and money from part-time work as money toward debt reduction. Although I do not agree with cutting out something you love, such as family holidays (we all need rejuvenation), to pay off a debt, I do believe you can budget, using the monthly expense sheet provided in chapter 3. This way, you at least become cognizant of what you are spending monthly and yearly. That way, if there are areas that you find to be wasteful, you can cut these from your budget to free up money for investment and debt reduction.

The key is attitude! Indeed, each of us can certainly find areas where excess frivolity reigns supreme and over time every little bit helps towards paying off debt and keeping more of your share. Above all, understand this, only a motivated person who is tired of being lackadaisical with respect to unnecessarily "handing their money to other people" will take the time to have a good look at what they have been doing. It is these Boomers who will stop overspending or overpaying for goods and services, who will decide upon realistic and workable solutions to reduce debt and who will thus, free up more money for the creation of long-term wealth.

As a final point, let us discuss value as it relates to keeping your share. In *Tips From The Top* I wrote a chapter entitled "The Truth About Commissions". In it we looked at value with respect to paying a professional to invest your money. Basically, no load equals no advice. Therefore, if you are a highly skilled, veteran investor with access to reliable, up-to-date, research, have an expert understanding of financial markets, know many of the stocks and bonds and can navigate your way through over one thousand mutual funds, then you probably do not need any help. If, however, you are a busy Baby Boomer with imperative financial goals and a desire to see your portfolio grow significantly, then professional advice on an ongoing basis is a necessity. The important word here is "professional" advice. In any industry there are outstanding, thoughtful professionals and there are "hucksters" who are trying to turn a buck and who put their personal best interest ahead of the customer's. To keep your share you must avoid these people. Here's how.

In my opinion, you have taken the first step by simply, reading this book. For the consumer, knowledge is power. The financial "huckster" does not want to see informed and intelligent people come into his or her office. Instead, this person prefers an individual who is ignorant in all financial matters and who refuses to even attempt to learn. Do not take this to mean that if you are not interested in financial planning that you are destined to fail financially. Instead, what it means is that you have no way of gauging your advisor and your investment portfolio against what is actually available. There are, for example, over one thousand mutual funds so why are yours among the best? If they are all from one fund family, why is that fund company superior to every other company on the market? Should you have a mix? Staying with our example, in the case of Mutual Funds, there are several excellent Mutual Fund Guides on the market. These guides allow the consumer to mathematically and categorically discern between the good, the bad and the mediocre. All of that said, quality, advice and people cost money.

Through your knowledge base in the area of investing, you will be able to decide if the value is there with respect to the return on your investment and the quality of the relationship that you have with your professional. If the quality is not there, fire him or her! That is also part of keeping your share. Remember, you have the right to demand strong returns. Indeed, since you may have only fifteen years or so before retirement, an additional 2% compounded annually over these years (in the case of a $100,000 RRSP), will give you an additional $156,700 on which to retire! For this reason, how your advisor chooses your investments is important, especially for the Boomer who would like to retire with some level of comfort. Also, if you are paying an extra 2% per year in "unnecessary commissions" due to a bad choice of advisor, your result is the same as choosing an inferior investment. Only an understanding of investing, in general, will prevent you from losing to lower returns in the case of bad investment choices, or from losing to selfishness in the case of being overcharged to invest. Thus, the responsibility of keeping your share starts with your personal responsibility. It starts with you. To keep your share, there is little need to be anxious. Instead, be intelligent, aware and informed. These are traits that so many of today's Baby Boomers already possess. Moreover, Boomers are a successful lot so, to keep your share, just be yourself and be aware of what is going on around you as it relates to your personal finances. Understand a little bit about tax and watch the federal budget on television each year. Start by being somewhat mindful about what is coming in and going out of your personal bank accounts each month and pay attention to the "nonsensical spending" that holds you back from paying off debt and building long-term wealth. In addition, read and ask questions so that you will be informed enough to align yourself with one of the many first-rate investment firms and advisors in Canada. As investors in this country, you are blessed with a highly skilled, highly regulated investment industry that is consistently seeking to improve itself. From a professional, as well as from a consumer standpoint, I am proud to be a part of this industry. In order to take advantage of the many investment options available to you, do some homework, as it is this that will give you peace of mind and help you to achieve superior investment returns. I recently overheard a financial planner who was griping about losing a client to a large brokerage firm. He said in disdain, "That client just wants high rates of return!" To which I thought, "No kidding!" Although the advisor-client relationship is very important, it comes second to the importance of realizing competitive returns on your portfolio. Some people stay in a relationship with an advisor because "he's a nice guy" or, because the investor has not taken the time to consider what else is available. So, again, do not get upset when it comes to keeping your share, instead, get informed.

"There is only one class of people that thinks more about money than the rich, and that is the poor. In fact, the poor can think of nothing else."

Oscar Wilde.

CHAPTER 7

HOW DO I KEEP UP?

Do you actually believe that our future and that of our children can possibly resemble the enlightened and dangerous existence of the characters in "Star Trek", or that technological advancements will resemble those in "Star Wars"? Since 1969, my grandmother (who is now ninety-eight years old), has told me repeatedly that my late grandfather was very fond of comic books. His particular favourites were those that depicted space travel and the adventures of "Flash Gordon". Although he passed away in the fifties, he used to argue that one day space travel would be a reality and that people would travel to other planets. This usually met with tremendous laughter and a recommendation from his friends to "Lay off the comics!" In 1969, when astronaut Neil Armstrong walked on the moon and proclaimed, "One small step for man, one giant leap for mankind", my grandmother could not help but think of her husband and smile.

Although our preoccupation with the future and space travel is exciting, if we are to be completely honest, we must admit that it is also a little disarming and even frightening. Imagine the time machine for a moment. You are propelled back to 1966, to the familiarity of your childhood or teenage years. After a day or two in awe of actually being there you begin to adapt to, and even take advantage of your situation (possibly even prophesying like a contemporary Rasputin). Now go forward thirty years to 2027. Think about what you may see and experience. As capable as you are in 1997, could you operate a vehicle that routinely and safely travels at 450 miles per hour? Would you have an anxiety attack upon entering one of "New" Toronto's posh restaurants, ordering your usual "rib eye and potatoes" (as you are admonished for being a barbarian) only to be served a small plate of rice, beans, vegetables and water? What about the clothes that you are wearing "circa 1997"? It may be similar to a person wearing a "zoot" to an elegant dinner party today. Clearly, you are out of touch, out of your element and at a very distinct disadvantage! Now, are you excited? Chances are you are terrified because you have not evolved into this new world along with everyone else. Instead, this world has passed you by. To me, very little else is more unsettling.

Yet this is the way that some Baby Boomers choose to invest. In the area of investments, changes are happening constantly. Although it is not imperative that you keep up with each one, as this is your advisor's job, a reasonable grasp of the changing landscape is advantageous. This understanding will help the Boomer who is intent on retiring comfortably to make strong and thoughtful, ongoing decisions. Another area of concern, or excitement, is when a significant change happens in an existing investment. Has one of the companies you hold created a new product? Has the president of the company died? More common today would be, has your portfolio manager, one who has served your mutual fund well, moved on and should you follow this individual? These are just a couple of changes that could take place and consequently impact your retirement goals positively or negatively.

If you were to look in the business section of any credible newspaper on any given day you would be amazed at the listing of all of the individual stocks, bonds, GICs, mutual funds, commodities and other specialized investments. Take the time to scan through this section and test yourself in regard to how many of these investments you can "decipher" and actually recognize. Can you find your own company stock, (assuming that your firm is publicly traded)? In the mutual fund section alone, you will find over one thousand offerings! Which of these investments has a strong track record and strong prospects for the future? Which of these investments will propel you into an outstanding retirement over the next fifteen years? Do you have enough information to make these decisions and, if not, are you willing to venture a "guess" when something as important as "thirty years in retirement" is at stake?

How do I keep up? This is becoming an increasingly important question for the busy Boomer and I understand it well because, like you, I am a busy professional. I am also a husband, a father of three daughters, a gardener, a housekeeper (although my wife could make a good argument to the contrary), an athlete, a "taxi service", a cheerleader, a dog walker, a person who does community service; and depending on what time it is, an array of other roles. Does this sound familiar? To most Baby Boomers my existence may actually seem very simplistic. Indeed, you might be saying to yourself, "No wonder he has time to write books, he isn't busy at all compared to me". Still, the question remains, given the Boomer's busy lifestyle, where does one find the twenty hours per week in order to keep up with an investment portfolio? The answer is simple, learn where to find the information quickly and efficiently so that you need spend only minutes per day.

The first obvious exercise is to read. A few weeks ago, I was going through some old notes from seminars I had attended over the years, and came across a great saying. It simply said, "All Leaders Are Readers". Our planet, as most Boomers have realized in this, the age of information, belongs to the informed. Thus for quick and efficient business and investment information, I would start each day scanning three publications. First, your best local newspaper's business section for the information that will inform you of local opportunities that you may examine and follow easily and firsthand. Next, scan the business section of a strong, national paper, such as *The Globe & Mail* or *The Toronto Star*. Look for articles that interest you, the hot stories of the day and locate your holdings in the stock, bond and mutual fund listings. Finally, scan *The Financial Post* in much the same fashion, looking for important information that affects you personally. *The Financial Post* has a very strong Mutual Fund section and you can examine a new fund rather closely almost every day. In addition, most newspapers now feature a special "fund ranking" section at least once per month.

This exercise should not take you any more than forty-five minutes to one hour per day. For a longer view of investing, go to your local bookstore. In the area of financial planning books, such as this one, there are many. As a reader, you should read books that are written for your own level of expertise and evolve to other books as you become more sophisticated. Nothing turns me off a subject more than initially getting in "over my head". Some of the more popular financial authors include: Gordon Pape, David Chilton, Nualla Beck, Peter Lynch (one of my favourites), George Soros and of course, anything written about the world's greatest investor, Warren Buffet, is a must-read.

In addition to general financial planning books, there is an array of specialty financial books. For example, there are now books specifically written so that the layperson can achieve an understanding of subjects such as commodities, specific stock trading strategies and offshore investing. Books that I believe are extremely valuable to Baby Boomers include the new array of Mutual Fund Guides that are updated yearly. I specifically like these books for Boomers because, as a generation, we are literally "pouring money" into Mutual Funds towards our retirement.

These Mutual Fund Guides will allow you, almost at a glance, to see how your funds have performed against their peer group over a short or protracted period of time. In *Ranga Chand's World Of Mutual Funds* each fund is broken down by company in the back of the book. Here you will find each categorized as "a heavy hitter", "an underachiever", "rookie class" or with no classification, which in my opinion means "O.K." or "mediocre", and "you can certainly do better than that". Again, some of the popular authors to look for here are Jonathan Chevreau (of *The Financial Post*), Gordon Pape and Duff Young.

In respect to accessing technology for a more up-to-date view, particularly in relation to Mutual Funds, you could purchase a subscription to Bell Charts or The Southam Rankings. Both of these programs are updated on a monthly basis and their purpose is to categorize and rank all Mutual Funds, best to worst, over prescribed periods of time. As I have stated many times in the past, all portfolio managers are not created equally! Thus, you will find that, in each category, some funds have five-year, compound returns of 4% per year, while others in the same area have performed at better than 20% per year over the same time period! Programs such as Bell Charts and Southam will show you these statistics. It is also important to note that because funds are so popular, particularly among us Boomers, strong competition in the "fund ranking business" is emerging. The result is precise, easy-to-understand information for you, the investor. Clearly, the busy, professional Boomer can get investment information very quickly when he or she is employing the use of a computer, some easy to read software, your local high quality bookstore and daily newspapers.

Now allow me to introduce to you by far the best resource you have at your disposal for up to date financial and investment information, your own financial advisor and his or her firm. Do you have any idea of the quantity and in most cases, the quality of the information that investment advisors and their firms can consistently produce? It is absolutely staggering! A strong, two-way relationship with a financial advisor will open up all of those learning opportunities to you. Even if you are a busy professional with a family to care for, you can "screen" the information you receive from your advisor. It is imperative that you build a relationship with an investment professional because, over time, he or she will understand what is pertinent to you and what is not. A word of caution though, financial advisors are often wise to the individual who opens a very small account with his or her firm and harbours the intention of a "do it yourself approach" with the lion's share of one's money. This individual then proceeds to constantly probe the advisor and the firm for information and expensive research reports. When financial planning practices are based on integrity, this type of "client" will be either shown the door or, at the very least, treated with the same respect that they are according their advisor. The way to receive all of the knowledge that you want, and more, is simply by building a professional relationship based on trust, integrity and a teamwork approach to one common goal. That goal is usually building long-term wealth for the Baby Boomer, and if done correctly, for that person's family.

Information from the financial advisor can come in two forms: verbal and written. Your advisor may call you at any given time to discuss changes to existing investments or new opportunities. You may want this information backed up by something in writing or a brochure and it is your right to insist that the information sent to you is understandable. From the advisor and his or her firm, you can expect to receive regular portfolio updates and reviews, quarterly newsletters, invitations to seminars and events, research reports as they are needed, information and prospectuses, annual reports concerning the investments you hold and ideas on new investments, as well as other opportunities that will allow you to continue to learn. Clearly, there is a strong push in the financial community to educate clients and the public at large. Regardless, it is up to you, the busy Boomer, to take advantage of this wealth of information. Remember, the cost of ignorance can be devastating. Without the ability to make strong decisions, you may accidentally own a portfolio that is averaging 6% per year when it could average double that amount with no further risk.

When Sir John Templeton was asked whom he felt would go down in history as the most important or significant person of the twentieth century his response was, Ronald Reagan. To paraphrase, Sir John argued that because "he stopped the cold war...billions of dollars could be diverted away from weapons and could be put into the economy in much more productive ways". Throughout his terms in office as the President of the United States, Reagan was known as "the great 'delegator' ". Indeed, there are those who believe that his greatest strength lay in his ability to empower his subordinates. Today, many Baby Boomers are business owners and managers and thus, understand the power of effective delegation. To efficiently keep up with the investment world, I recommend that you continue to use this trait of delegation. You do not have to go to a library and "dig" in 1997. Instead, use journalists, authors, computer programs, the internet, investment firms, mutual fund companies and your personal financial advisor to bring the information to you. They all want you to have the most current information so that you may make strong decisions in this, the last half of your working life. Try not to be too hard on yourself. You do not have to, nor are you expected to, know everything. However, just as our desire is to have a working knowledge of hockey (for our children's sake if nothing else) I recommend you spend at least as much effort each year keeping yourself informed of changes in the financial landscape. This way you won't find yourself at your first Toronto Maple Leaf game in several years looking for your favorite player Lanny McDonald, or asking your next door neighbour, "what is a Mutual Fund?"

"If a man empties his purse into his head, no one can take it from him."

Benjamin Franklin.

CHAPTER 8

THE EXTRA PUSH TO WEALTH: "THE TRILLION DOLLAR GENERATION"

So, you are forty five years old, you have saved nothing, you do not have a pension plan and frankly, you are frightened. Is there enough time to move forward if I begin to save today? Is it already too late? Considering that we do not have much money left over at the end of each month, how will we ever be able to retire? If this is your story, there is a possibility that you will have a major problem at age sixty-five. On the other hand, perhaps your parents, grandparents or a well-to-do aunt will "save your bacon"! Indeed, financially speaking, the "cavalry" might be on its way in the form of an inheritance. I must first apologize, for I certainly do recognize and respect the fact that someone must first pass away in order for your personal economics to benefit. However, demographics indicate that many in our "aging population" will pass on over the next fifteen years. Thus I want you to be prepared, with solid investment knowledge in relation to how you should properly invest.

A few years ago I had a client who received a $60,000 inheritance from her father. She is married with two children and neither her, nor her husband has a significant pension. At the time, she was thirty-six years old and could only afford to invest a small amount monthly. This inheritance could have (and should have) been the family's financial salvation and the beginning of long term wealth. I went to see her but she put me off, asking me to return in a month while she "got her head together". When I did return, the family had two new cars in the driveway, a big screen TV and had just booked a southern vacation. She invested the remaining $2,500 with me. Assuming an average annual growth rate on a strong investment of 12% per year over twenty-nine years, her $2,500 will be worth $66,875, when she is sixty-five. Let us suppose instead, that her commitment was financial independence, rather than instant gratification. In this scenario, seventy-five percent of the inheritance was invested, leaving twenty-five percent for "fun". The results would be $45,000 invested at 12% compounding annually for the same twenty-nine years, or $1,203,750!!! This woman's reality and that of her family would have been different especially as one approaches retirement when gauged against $66,000! Also, think about the benefactor for a moment. I am a father of three daughters. My wife Tracy and I are certainly not building long-term, generational wealth so as to provide our children with simple, mindless "fun" such as cars and TV sets, only to envision them retiring poorly due to immaturity, poor planning and selfishness. I say selfishness because in our example it is possible that perhaps this woman's father wanted her to build wealth, use it and then pass it on to her children, his grandchildren. He certainly did not save money all of his life so that his grandchildren could play Nintendo on a forty-five inch screen! What if the education of his grandchildren had been his goal? On an investment of $2,500 this will be difficult to achieve.

Does all of this seem harsh? If so, I make no apologies. Read any material on the Baby Boomer generation and you will see that the floodgates of inheritance are going to open. It will be emotional as you are losing a loved one, but from a wealth building standpoint, you will have the opportunities your relative desires for you. We have been called the "trillion dollar generation", meaning that approximately one trillion dollars could conceivably be inherited in Canada over the next fifteen years or so. Are you getting any of this money? Many of whom I speak to, do not believe that they are. Without a doubt, they will be surprised to learn what I already know. "What I already know" is that your parents, whom you believe are on a fixed pension and are just getting by, are in fact very conservative, and secretly quite well off. In the seniors social strata showing your wealth is generally a "no-no". Seniors are socially conservative and in many cases secretive; even to (and sometimes especially to) their own children. Stop and think about it. Many of these people grew up in the depression and have learned to "stretch a dollar". Furthermore, in some cases, they were saving money for forty years. Upon their death many of you will be shocked to see that your parents were not only saving money but were doing it properly. You will find that they had a financial advisor, stocks, bonds and high performing mutual funds. Moreover, they did not spend all of their time playing bridge and enjoying lawnbowling. I know for a fact that many of my own senior clients are extremely astute investors. However, modesty and the desire for confidentiality conceals this fact. All of this may mean that you could have an unexpected inheritance coming your way between now and retirement. So, just in case, let's build a tentative game plan concerning how you should go about investing this legacy.

Unless you have an incredible and immediate opportunity that happens to be sitting in front of you, my first piece of advice upon receiving an inheritance and assuming a fast probate, is to do nothing for a month. This is new money to you and as such it is probably a good idea to place it in a thirty day deposit so that you can make some concrete plans. Next, call a financial advisor for a new, full review of your updated financial position. This will give you and your advisor an updated "snapshot" of where you are financially. After analyzing your position as well as establishing your new financial goals, determine how much money, after inflation it will take to achieve what you would like. Take into account all of your present investments as well as the inheritance. At this point, allot a percentage for long-term growth and wealth building as well as a certain amount for "fun". Without a doubt, be realistic when discussing this situation. For a while now, you may have had your eye on a boat, a certain car or a dream vacation and, as long as it only takes up ten or fifteen percent of your inheritance, what is the harm? Depending on what you have done in the past from an investment standpoint, budgeting for a little bit of fun may be more than reasonable. As for the rest of the money it is best, particularly in the case of a Baby Boomer who has high economic standards and the retirement clock ticking, to invest as much and as prudently as possible. Do you remember the day that your son or daughter was born? Look at them now! This is how quickly retirement will be upon us and you will certainly want long term security then.

At this point, you and your financial advisor will have determined your long-term goals and how much money you will be investing towards realizing these goals. You should also be taking a strong look at tax implications and your options with respect to saving and deferring tax over the next many years. From an investment standpoint, you should look at investing your inheritance as follows:

1. Maximize the unused portion in your RRSP. Depending on your situation with respect to your marital status, pensions and existing investments, you may choose some or all of the investment as a spousal RRSP. Also, examine your tax position to see what amount you should invest into your RRSP in the first year of the inheritance so as to best use tax to your advantage.

2. With the remaining money, if there is any remaining money after your RRSP investment, invest in a balanced port-

folio, again being aware of the tax implications of investing outside your RRSP. Although I will not go into detail here, you should speak to your advisor about the differences between interest bearing, dividend bearing and capital gain bearing investments. Also, have this person explain (to your satisfaction) the risk and volatility of each proposed non-registered investment.

3. Another option for Boomers who are still saddled with a mortgage, is to use your inheritance to pay off the mortgage and get a home equity line of credit for the amount that you have just paid off. Although you will still continue to make the payment to your bank, in return, you now have a lump sum to invest in equities and mutual funds. In addition, as we have learned in previous chapters, interest on an investment loan is tax deductible, yet this same payment, when it was a mortgage was not deductible. Now you are not only using your inheritance but also utilizing the equity in your home, using the bank and our government as an ally to fund your retirement plan.

As always, whether it be in the form of a tax benefit from RRSPs or other vehicles, a big gain can be realized from yearly reinvestment of refunds, so it is a great habit to practice!

Last year, I remember reading a statement by Ed Howe, that said, "Don't take up a man's time talking about the smartness of your children, he wants to talk about the smartness of his children". Truly, it is absolutely fascinating, as a parent, to try to conceive the power of the love we feel for our children. While some of our older investors state emphatically, and sometimes facetiously that they are spending their kid's inheritance, and, "Let them get their own damn money," I secretly believe that some type of financial legacy is important to most people. Almost everyone I know wants to see their children succeed. As such, without putting themselves in financial jeopardy, it is desirable to leave some money behind when money is no longer of use to them. Thus, is the interesting concept of inheriting generational wealth.

I would have been remiss if I had not devoted some time in this, a Baby Boomer's book, to the issues of inheritance and the "trillion dollar generation". For some, however, there really isn't some "secret nest-egg". In fact, earlier in this chapter some of you may have been frustrated. You may have been saying, "John, you don't understand, my parents are poor. Really!" In this case, the rest of this book is even more important to you. You must do the right things. As such your challenge, the challenge to build long-term wealth and security, is even greater. The good news is that others have done it before you. You may not receive a head start, but then this is true for many of us. Of even more concern is the individual who is given wealth only to meet it with disrespect and thus, lose it, not just for themself but for future generations. This is failure. If, you are fortunate enough to receive an inheritance, my advice to you is to respect it and utilize it. If on the other hand, your challenge is to be one hundred percent "self-made", you must build wealth through hard work, perseverance and by utilizing outstanding advice. Your victory will be just that much sweeter. Finally, whether your success is monetary or otherwise, it will be your own, as Voltaire said, "Whoever serves his country well has no need of ancestors". With all of our technology, global opportunities and our seemingly natural ability to succeed and prosper, this is the essence of the self made Boomer.

CHAPTER 9

"BECOMING THE MILLIONAIRE AT THE MALL" (or Living Within Your Means)

"You are only what you are when no one is looking."
Robert C. Edwards.

In the Boomer's adolescent years the music of the day was Jimi Hendrix, Janis Joplin, The Doors, The Beatles and Pink Floyd. To keep in touch with the music and symbols of many bands, fashion dictated minimalism. Long hair, unshaven faces, bare feet and a minimum of clothing were the styles of the sixties and early seventies. Indeed, if you ever watch a rerun of Columbo or Cannon even the so-called "establishment" (using Mod Squad jargon) was a little bit unkempt, complete with long sideburns and "long hair". As for the Boomer vehicles, most of us were satisfied with a car, period. For the avant-garde individual, however, there was the "Harley", the "Bug" or, for the romantic, the "VW Van".

The Boomer of 1997 has replaced this long forgotten lifestyle with the Lexus, the Armani suit and the designer haircut. I, of course, am one of those individuals who has been conditioned by the media to strive for the "good life". Most Baby Boomers I know, either as colleagues, clients or friends, have adopted over the years that same attitude of living with luxury. Of course, the problem occurs when that high-end lifestyle is adopted by people who cannot truly afford to live it. This, I believe, is a symptom of a society of Boomers who want desperately to appear very financially successful regardless of whether or not they are. The pressure to keep up appearances is everywhere today and, to some degree, is one of our leftover legacies from the eighties. In most cases credit is very easy, particularly, in the two-income household. I believe that this has created a society of impatient Boomers who want everything today, "while I'm still young enough to enjoy it".

Does this sound like a typical Baby Boomer couple discussing a new purchase? The husband, Peter, comes home at the end of a hard day in mid-June. His wife, Carla, is on the deck relaxing after a full day at the office.

Peter: "My goodness, what a hot one today!"

Carla: "Yeah, it's a killer! How was your day?"

Peter: "Brutal, it's good to be home; if it wasn't so hot. Is the air on in the house?"

Carla: "Yes, but I hate to be stuck inside. The Carson's just put in a pool."

Peter: "How can they afford that? They don't make as much as we do, do they?"

Carla: "I don't know! Maybe they got a good deal or maybe they got a low interest rate."

Peter: "We should look into it, I'd love a pool. It would really make great use of the yard. We wouldn't need a cottage then and the kids would use it every day! We could have friends over more often too. You know, we really don't use our yard as much as we should because it's just too hot!"

Carla: "Peter, we already owe $36,000 on the line of credit, our mortgage is high, we are barely contributing to our RRSPs; and the kids always need money. We can't afford a pool!"

Peter: "Maybe we could spread the payments out over ten years or something. If we don't do it now, we'll be too old to enjoy it. The kids need to learn how to swim and it's at this age that they'll get the most fun out of it, not in ten years when they are ready to leave home for university!"

Carla: "Well, what about university, how will we pay for that?!"

Peter: "We have good jobs, swimming in the yard will keep them out of trouble and probably help them to be better students. Also, I'm eventually going to get a promotion, Simmons is retiring in a few years and I'll get his job. We can save for their schooling then. Just call the place tomorrow. I can't take this heat!"

Carla: "I guess it wouldn't hurt to get an estimate. A pool would be nice to have."

Thus, upon the purchase of the pool, another $20,000 is heaped onto the debt load of another, unsuspecting Canadian family who are only guilty of wanting what they cannot afford in an attempt to keep up with the Jones', or in this case, the Carson's. Remember, attitude constitutes the greatest part of investing. It is gaining the maturity and the vision of a long-term investor. If the fear of a harsh retirement is your motivation, so be it. If, instead, you love the positive aspects of leisure this may be your driving force. Regardless of what moves you, if you are living above your means you must change immediately.

Steven Speilberg is a cool guy. Apart from the fact that he is "the director" of the Boomer generation, he also exemplifies, albeit as a much amplified version, the creativity and genius of many Baby Boomers. Indeed, he has fascinated us, and our children alike, with characters such as E.T., the Tyrannosaurus Rex in "Jurassic Park", Jaws, Indiana Jones, Roger Rabbit and of course, all of the riveting and disturbing characters in "Schlinder's List". Apart from Mr. Speilberg's creative gifts, he also projects a remarkably unpretentious appearance. I read an article on Speilberg a couple of years ago describing him as "the millionaire at the mall". The article went on to say that, with his easy going manner and usual "uniform" of jeans, running shoes, T-shirt and baseball cap, he could easily be mistaken for any Baby Boomer out at the local Gap store looking for clothes for his kids. I thought to myself, "What an interesting image for an extremely successful person". Not only is he (and actually a growing number of wealthy Boomers) not showing off his wealth, he seems to be motivated by the actual work that he does so well. This is a throwback to the "old days" where things such as modesty, quality and humility were not only in vogue but were common. Certainly, this is a much more common and much more practical approach to life than living way above your means simply to appear successful.

Our finance minister Paul Martin has stated that, "We are in hock up to our eyeballs". Many of us Boomers, upon hearing this, bang our fists, curse the government and ask in mock disgust, "How could they have put us in this position!" An hour later that same person is using an already overloaded credit card, with no intention of paying off the monthly balance, simply because he or she "needs" something.

Where did this notion of minimalism become lost? When, exactly, did it fall out of fashion? Clearly, I am not suggesting that you sell your boat, your Mercedes, scale down your home and live like Theodore Kazcynsky! I am asking you, instead, to analyze your present position, become more cognizant of your everyday expenses and to consider putting off instant pleasures (to some degree) so that you will have enough cash flow to build long-term wealth. Sadly, many of today's Boomers have developed habits similar to those of their parents. This is the habit of being "asset rich and cash poor".

Simply put, this "affliction" represents the lifestyle of one who lives for today and lives above their means.

Symptomatic of this style of "financial planning" is a couple (or individual) who has worked for thirty-five or forty years, owns their home, their cars, their furniture, a boat, a cottage (which they intend to keep in the family), several other "toys" but with little cash on hand. The Baby Boomer cannot fall into this trap for a couple of obvious reasons. The first of these is our concern about the strength and longevity of the Canada Pension Plan and the second is the ease with which large corporations change the rules with respect to length of employment and benefits. In my opinion, the Boomer must have a personal portfolio of his or her own and consider these pensions "gravy". A portfolio of any magnitude can only be built if one lives below their means. That is not to say that I am against "toys", just the opposite! Rather, my concern stems from people purchasing large items they cannot afford, particularly when it comes at the expense of not just long-term wealth, but at the expense of simple, long-term security.

It has been said in business, as well as in athletic circles, that "Winning is a habit, unfortunately so is losing". The habit of living above your means may be holding you back from building wealth as you move into retirement over the next fifteen or twenty years.

Permit me then to give you some advice and suggest some strategies designed to help you break the losing habit of overspending and ultimately put all of your new-found investment knowledge to work.

Step #1: Work with a financial advisor to design some important financial goals. Again, as we have discussed in earlier chapters, these should be "your goals", not those of your advisor. You have to be the one who is motivated by these objectives so it should not matter what your advisor wants to do with his or her life. Take plenty of time on this exercise. I believe that it is invaluable because, when coupled with a solid, overall financial plan, a Boomer can clearly determine what must be done to reach financial goals, such as tax saving, children's education or retirement planning. The most valuable adjunct to this idea though, is that you can now gauge each major purchase against investing towards your long-term goals and this puts short-term frivolity in an entirely different context.

Step#2: Update your net worth and operating (cash flow) statements at least once a year, and preferably twice per year. This will show you if you are getting closer to your long-term goals and how quickly it is happening. Looking at your cash flow consistently will determine positive or negative changes with respect to your monthly cash flow as well as keep you grounded in reality as to what you can and cannot presently afford.

Step #3: As a rule of thumb, no more than 20% of your cash flow should be going towards servicing debt. This will leave you money for monthly expenses such as food, clothes, and enable you to build an emergency fund as well as achieve short term goals such as the purchase of "toys". If you are willing to invest 20% of your cash flow into debt, you should certainly be open to investing at least that much into long term investments. However, this will not be a reality if you have a large percentage of your after tax earnings going to service short-term debt and a mortgage. When you reach that 20% level of debt, put the brakes on your purchases for a while.

Step #4: When purchasing big ticket items, shop the market. Quality will vary but when you are going to purchase a particular make and model of a product, stores will vary in price depending on their circumstances. Putting in the time can save you money on each purchase.

Step #5: Try not to compare yourself with others who you assume are in a similar financial position to yourself. Take the example of the couple purchasing the pool earlier in this chapter. Peter tried to justify the purchase by suggesting that "they were earning more than the Carson's". What the Carson's may not have let Peter in on was that they had just received a $500,000 inheritance or that, unlike Peter and Carla, they had not had a trip in ten years. Perhaps the Carson's are excellent savers or had shares in some stock that skyrocketed. Maybe they do not care about retirement and they have a "live for today" philosophy. My point is simply that people are private about their finances, and rightly so. Thus, your circumstances cannot be compared to your neighbour's, so do not bother trying.

Step #6: If you are wealthy, you can skip this step for it is aimed at those who must be constantly alert to spending in order to get ahead. Step # 6 is geared towards cutting corners. What I mean by this obvious statement is to list some items that you constantly purchase and decide if there are some you can do without. Perhaps you should forego lottery tickets, constant fast food junkets, cigarettes and unnecessary clothing which is being purchased by habit because you are at the mall anyway. Try not to purchase excessive jewelry, cut back on the number of dinners out and do not overspend on children in an attempt to win them over and amuse them. Finally, eliminate extravagant birthday and Christmas gifts for family and friends. It is interesting that some of the most affluent looking Christmas trees belong to the people who can least afford it. Most of our very wealthy friends give their children one or two gifts each and exchange names for "token gifts" with other family members. These are just a few items that come to mind and please, do not accuse me of being "miserly" because I am not. In fact, I had to ask some of my "miserly" colleagues to help me compile this list. (They have asked me to keep their names anonymous so that they may continue to be "cheap" to all of their relatives). The bottom line is to cut corners so that you can have that little bit extra to achieve your own goals. An extra $175 per month for example, after cutting corners for twenty years (compounding at 12% annually) will put an additional $169,468 into your personal portfolio.

Every person who is engaged in the practice of investing money for his or her future has one ultimate goal in mind, financial independence. This is a difficult and somewhat daunting thing to achieve and I say this because only a small percentage of our population have, or will reach, a level of independence that meets with their own satisfaction. While I do not agree with the unrealistic notion of sacrificing absolutely everything today for the sake of long-term investment, the idea of impatience among the Baby Boomer populace does not bode well for building long-term wealth. Ultimately, we must all find a middle ground. This philosophy of compromise will allow for living well, although not overtly extravagant, while at the same time providing a strong base and sufficient cash flow to build wealth. Moreover, it is compromise that will carry the Boomer into retirement and create the long term prosperity we all desire. To achieve this measure of wealth we must recognize the distinct difference between true wealth and the appearance of wealth as we move into the last half of our retirement planning cycle. Only investment and control of your finances will help you to become "the millionaire at the mall."

"I'd like to live like a poor man–only with lots of money."

Pablo Picasso.

CHAPTER 10

"SALLY'S DECIDED TO BECOME A Ph.D." Funding Your Children's Education.

Approximately one-half of Canada's millionaires do not possess post secondary education.

This is not to say that this group is uneducated, only that they have not attended college or university. In many cases, these individuals are self-taught, well read, savvy, street smart and brilliant and all without the benefit of advanced, formal schooling. This also indicates, however, that many of our most economically successful citizens are in fact, formally educated. In addition, education at the higher levels can hold a certain social and intrinsic appeal. Having said this, I know of very few parents who, regardless of their educational background, would not want their child to have the opportunity to attend a fine college or university. The problem in 1997 with respect to education, however, may simply be a question of a parent's economic position. The danger then becomes such that some of Canada's brightest and most motivated young people may not have the opportunity to learn at a level that is suitable to their ability. Personally, if I ever need major surgery, I would like to be able to assume that my surgeon is brilliant and not just fortunate enough to have had parents who were well heeled.

It has been reported that the cost of a four year university degree, including housing, is between approximately $48,000 and $56,000, although this varies depending on the institution and the province. The Baby Boomer of the mid-nineties is very concerned with the rising costs of education because, with respect to growth, they far surpass inflation. It was reported in an August 1996 *Toronto Star* article on this subject that the Canadian Scholarship Trust Foundation estimates tuition costs will grow at the startling rate of 10%, compounding each year! This would force tuition rates to double every seven years and the fact remains that these shocking statistics seem logical. Federal and Provincial governments have tightened the belt (so to speak) and the result will be much less support to post secondary institutions. This, of course, puts tremendous pressure on individual students and we as their parents, who are simultaneously building money for a comfortable retirement.

I do not have to expound on the pressure that Boomers face in educating their children. Boomers are in the age group where many of their children are in grade ten or eleven and are excitedly looking at their future opportunities. Many of these kids have worked hard, have sacrificed, grown as students and as people. As parents, when you look at them, your pride swells up and you feel good about how they have been raised and who they have become. They deserve to continue on in school! Your parents provided for your education and, if you were like me, in many ways you took it for granted then. Things are different now, much different. Education is no longer an inalienable right but rather an opportunity for the student and a distinct challenge for the parent, if total funding of your children's education is your goal.

So how can you approach this daunting task of giving your children the educational opportunity that they deserve? In short, it depends on your time line between now and when they begin post secondary studies, your commitment to building an education plan and your cash flow in relation to funding schooling while trying to fund other goals. However, here are a few ideas and I will break it down as: (A) Funding for Younger Children, for example, age 1 to 10 and (B) Funding for Older Children, for example, over 10 years old and much closer to post secondary age.

Funding For Younger Children

When planning for your child's education keep in mind the power of compound interest. Thus, obviously sooner is better. In the case of starting an education plan, whether it be formal or informal, it is best to open an account either at birth or shortly thereafter. The most important factor with respect to your planning, though, is that you do have options. The first option I would like to examine with you, is the

Registered Education Savings Plan or the RESP. This popular plan, which is recognized and approved by the government, earns interest on the investment inside the plan on a tax free basis. To open this plan, you purchase units according to what you and your financial advisor determine your education costs to be in the future. In this scenario, the age of the child when the plan is opened determines the monthly cost per unit to the parent. You can open an RESP until a child's thirteenth birthday and the age stipulation for the plan's use is that the student must be enrolled in post secondary studies by his or her twenty second birthday. In the first year of school, you as the parent, will receive back all of your deposits, minus fees, tax free. In the second year of studies and every year thereafter, the student will receive money directly to him or her and this amount is fully taxable to the student. An important drawback to the RESP that you must understand is that if your child does not attend post secondary education, you receive back only your net principle and you forfeit your interest. Over the long term this can be very substantial. It is also important to consider how money is invested over the long-term. Indeed, RESPs are not invested in equities and although this may appear "safe", I believe that most competent financial advisors could make the argument that, over the long term, blue chip equities have a far better chance of keeping pace with inflation and thus, the skyrocketing cost of education.

Another way of investing for your children's education is through the aforementioned equities. This would be either in high quality, global equity funds or in a blue chip stock portfolio. This portfolio will fluctuate, but in my opinion, is probably the only vehicle that will have a chance of keeping up with the continuously inflating prices of post secondary school. If you choose a formal trust account for your children, you should discuss this option and the cost with your lawyer.

A very common and effective way of funding schooling is to invest in a non-registered portfolio, held separately in the parents names or in the lower income earner's name. Taxes will have to be paid by one or both parents but there are some distinct advantages. First, you can invest using small monthly amounts and add lump sums as you wish or as relatives such as grandparents wish. In addition, the choice of how to invest is totally up to you. In the end you can achieve outstanding rates of return, defer taxes through capital gains and diversify globally, while maintaining control of this money throughout your child's post secondary career. I believe that the most important advantage to this plan is its flexibility. Indeed, because this is an "informal" education plan set up between you and your financial advisor, if your child does not attend post secondary school you may keep the money yourself, allow the child to continue the investment towards his or her own retirement, help your child to buy a first home, assist the child in starting a business, or in any other imaginable venture. In other words, you are in possession of a large lump sum of money that, although, not used for school can be used for anything you desire.

Using straight mathematics and arbitrarily using 8% as the figure that might possibly be realistic in gauging the rising costs of education, let's look at how this would work if your child is two years old today and you wish to fully fund a four year education in sixteen years.

All Approximations

Today's cost of four years of university = $48,000

"Possible" cost in 16 years (8% compound inflation which is a "guess" based on recent figures)
= $164,448.

Investing $3,480 per year or $290/month for 16 years at 12% compound growth = $166,636.

Be sure to keep in mind that although $290 per month per child looks unmanageable for many young Canadian families, this amount will seem smaller when gauged against inflation over time. (At 4% compound inflation, $290 in sixteen years would equal $154 in 1997.) Thus, my advice, if these figures are not possible, is to start with what you can afford. As your circumstances change positively, due to other areas of financial planning, you can increase your commitment to your children's education.

Funding For Older Children

In this scenario the task is more difficult. However, if you have done some other things right, such as pay off your mortgage, built a successful business or received promotions and thus, a higher income, you may be all right. In many households, the money that was previously earmarked for a now retired mortgage is spent directly on saving and paying for post secondary education while the child is attending university. Another effective method of funding for older children is giving the task to one particular parent thus opting to put a good portion of a second income towards paying for school. Another possibility, as was stated in earlier chapters is an inheritance. Should inheritances be forthcoming and whether or not the inheritance goes directly to your children or to yourself, a portion of this money would certainly be well invested in a child's education. Realistically, if you have done nothing and you have teenage children, you are "behind the eight ball", so to speak. I have, however, given you three options and I am certain that when your child's future is on the line you can be quite creative. If part time and summer jobs are available to your child, you may be involved in a joint venture with respect to funding education.

While it may be a stretch to get all of our brightest young people through, we must, although it is difficult to imagine paying $100,000 or more for one's post secondary education. I, like many of you, sincerely hope that this will not become a reality. Perhaps, if costs do become excessive, corporate sponsorship will be available. Regardless, money must be built up at home in some form as a means of giving children this start because, if no financial plans are made, you may one day hear the statement that should fill your heart with pride, but instead creates fear, "Sally has decided to become a Ph.D."

CHAPTER 11

INVESTING AS AN ENTREPRENEUR

If you are an entrepreneur, the main thing you must understand with respect to investing is that you must. Entrepreneurial Boomers have every opportunity to build wealth and while we are in an enviable position with respect to the ability to make our fortune free of a salary cap, we are also in the dangerous position of being without a retirement "safety net". Indeed, we cannot depend on a large corporation helping to fund our ultimate retirement. Upon retirement many of us may choose to sell our business, others may wish to pass it on to our children, but regardless, additional money will be required upon retirement. As you read this you may beg to differ, believing that you "have worked hard to build a successful business and that this will fund your retirement". Perhaps it will and perhaps your business will be obsolete in 15 years. Perhaps your business will not have what you perceive its value to be and that ultimately your lifestyle will necessitate more money than your business is worth. Let me give you an example. Let us suppose that you are accustomed to living on $250,000 per year. In order to generate this sum from investments each year you will need to have approximately $2.8 million ($2,800,000 x 9% income =$252,000 per year) invested! Has your business been valued at this much?

As in the case of your everyday business life, your investment life calls for 100% self-responsibility. Moreover, given the fast-paced lifestyle characteristic of an entrepreneur, it is crucial that you work with an outstanding financial advisor who understands your business and your specific needs with respect to building your retirement plan. Remember, there is no corporate "safety net" so you must succeed. To help you succeed, a good financial advisor must be able to recognize liquidity and cash flow needs as well as the seasonal nature of your business and how this can affect your investment style.

If you have not yet read, or do not yet subscribe to, *Success* magazine, I recommend that you begin doing so as it contains valuable ideas and encouragement for every entrepreneur. This magazine frequently profiles, and shares the wisdom of, successful entrepreneurs such as "Virgin's" Richard Branson; and "Calloway Golf's" Eli Calloway. I maintain that "knowledge is power", and as such I believe this magazine is important for small to medium-sized business owners. Using my back issues of *Success*, as well as my experience in advising my own entrepreneurial clients, I have come up with a list of ideas that I believe acknowledge the unique position of the people who drive today's economy and may continue to do so in the future.

1. Maintain a short-term reserve of six to twelve months of capital to support slow periods in your business.

2. Invest as much as possible whenever you have it.

3. Employ a "team" that includes a financial advisor, accountant and lawyer.

4. Maximize your RRSPs and leverage only if it does not restrict your ability to borrow against your business.

Before I elaborate on each of these points, let me make it clear to you that I personally respect no one person more than the one who can break through his or her fears of having no "safety-net" and stand-up and be counted with their entrepreneurial peers. Without a doubt the business owner is the wealthiest person on the planet both monetarily and from the standpoint of professional and personal growth. This incentive must exist or there would be no incentive to take the risk. This hard-earned wealth is to be applauded and what follows is some advice aimed at making the most of your opportunity.

Build A Serious Short-Term Reserve

Often good businesses go under because they lack the capital required to see entrepreneurs through inevitable business slow-downs. The first rule of financial planning is to have anywhere from 6 to 12 months of operating capital in a separate account. These funds could then be used to pay your bills, your staff and your salary.

Because it is short-term in nature it needs to be liquid and as such the vehicles used should be money market funds, short-term bonds, term deposits and cash. Your accountant will tell you when the account has grown past what is necessary, and of course, you can invest this excess amount into your business' technology or into your investment portfolio.

Invest As Much As Possible When You Can

Financially speaking, entrepreneurs are a special breed. Moreover, as a Boomer, your business may not be mature enough to enjoy a steady and predictable cash flow. In some cases your work may be seasonal. For example, last summer you and your staff sacrificed weekends and worked fourteen-hour days to build 288 decks. If there is room for extravagance, go ahead and splurge! Perhaps a new car or a trip to Europe is in order, but regardless, do not forget your investment portfolio! Purchase your RRSP now, or, if your advisor does not think that it is a good time to buy stocks, put the money in a cash account and act when the markets are right. The key is to get the money out of your hands immediately or your RRSP might suddenly appear as a boat or snowmobile.

Build A Cohesive Financial "Team"

Imagine a top-notch lawyer, accountant and financial advisor all working together to understand your business, your personal finances as well as your business and personal objectives. Their purpose is to help you, their client, achieve wealth. Does this not sound like a team that you would like to have working on your behalf? So why is it such a rare phenomenon? In a word, ego! Many professionals have pride and egos and each person believes they know what is right for you. Your task then is to interview people and take the time to bring together a team of professionals. Synergy must be your goal. For example, remove from your list a lawyer who, despite being outstanding, is a "control freak" and know-it-all. Furthermore, make it clear to your potential advisors that although you want their advice, you also want them to work with other consultants who bring additional skills to the team. Each should know their role. The accountant is responsible for the books and taxes, lawyers deal with estates, wills and all legal issues, while the financial advisor invests your money. While it is true that this team will cost you time and money, remember that you are building long-term, generational wealth and so it is worth it.

Maximize Your RRSP

As I constantly state, RRSPs are a "great deal" and all Canadians should maximize their RRSPs if possible. When you sell your business, most of the proceeds will go into a non-registered account and these funds will be a wonderful addition to an already solid RRSP. Moreover, both areas should be income-split. This strategy will help you build a large lump sum as well as create wealth outside your business.

Borrowing for an investment (leveraging, as previously discussed), is a viable option for Boomer-entrepreneurs who wish to save tax and build a non-registered portfolio. Prior to taking any action, I recommend meeting with all members of your team to evaluate risk and reward from the standpoint of investment options and whether or not they are affordable. The impact of cash flow and your ability to borrow for upcoming opportunities within your business will also need to be taken into consideration.

In closing this chapter, I would suggest that although intelligent investing is universal, the challenges and opportunities of the entrepreneur are unique to the evolution of their business. Your "team" should be able to recognize this fact and be sensitive to the changing climate of your business, whatever it may be.

CHAPTER 12

EVEN MORE "TIPS FROM THE TOP"
Wisdom from Fellow Boomers

I am truly excited! In *Tips From The Top*, I brought together 50 of the best thinkers in Canadian and international investing. Here, in a chapter entitled "Wisdom from Fellow Boomers", I offer you some advice from four of Canada's most outstanding and well-known Boomers who are in the business of building wealth. Please allow me to introduce you to these individuals who are, arguably, among Canada's best-known financial experts.

Thane Stenner has been Midland Walwyn's number one Financial Advisor for the past three years. Thane is a Senior Vice President and Director at Midland and he heads the Stenner Team of Whiterock

B.C. Outside of running one of the most successful practices in the industry, Thane and his wife, Darci (also a Financial Advisor) have three young children. They understand the life of the busy Baby Boomer.

Bill Sterling is the Global Strategist for the U.S. "powerhouse", BEA Associates out of New York. Bill is a Boomer with an absolutely outstanding resumé. As a former international economist with Merrill Lynch, Bill introduced global investment as a three dimensional chess game with the winners being those who could simultaneously monitor interest rates, exchange rates, and equity valuations that influence bonds, equities and currencies. Bill holds an M.A. and a Ph.D. from Harvard University and is a portfolio advisor to C.I.'s Global, Global Equity RSP, International Balanced and International Balanced RSP funds. C.I., as many of you already know (through your own holdings), employs a group of extremely strong money managers and I am honoured to include Bill in this chapter.

Neil Murdoch knows emerging markets. Indeed, as a lead manager at A.I.C. for the A.I.C. Emerging Markets Fund, he must. A.I.C. is located in Hamilton, Ontario and, growing up in this city, I derived a particular thrill in watching them grow into a money management "powerhouse". Allow me, if you will, to go out on a limb and predict that as a firm, A.I.C., will be the next "Trimark" in Canada. Certainly, upon meeting the quality of individuals among their money managers, one would have difficulty disputing this claim. The extent to which Mr. Murdoch has played a role in the success of A.I.C. will be made clear as you read through his quality contribution to this chapter.

In his essay, Neil will explain why Boomers need the long term aggressive growth of emerging markets and how these investments can be an important part of a Boomer's portfolio.

Sue Dabarno is the President of Midland Walwyn's Atlas Capital. Ms. Dabarno is responsible for the overall success of Atlas and she has employed some of the truly great money managers to help carry out her mission. On the global side, Atlas has Bill Dodge, a well known money manager who you may have seen interviewed on CNN or other major U.S. stations. Managing the Canadian emerging markets for Sue, is "superstar manager", Wayne Deans of Deans-Knight in Vancouver. Collaborating with Sue on this article is Doug Knight, a great bond manager, a Baby Boomer and the other part of money manager Deans Knight. I am pleased to include Sue, a fellow Baby Boomer, as a contributor as she is one of the most focused individuals at Midland Walwyn.

I encourage you to heed the "Wisdom of Fellow Boomers" and so follows their insight.

The Tax Smart Investor
By Thane Stenner

As an experienced Financial Advisor to individual investors and their families, I see a lot of people who are interested in improving their investment returns. Unfortunately, many investors tend to think too short-term and only consider an investment based on its reported total return in the newspaper or some "Top 10" research report. Generally speaking, investors are becoming more educated, especially in regards to how their investments are being taxed and the advantages of dividends and capital gains over interest income, and that's good. But I would like to go one step further and discuss how a "buy and hold" investment strategy is really the best of all worlds when it comes to money.

Investors should never make an investment decision without considering the effect of taxes on their investment returns. I've borrowed an example and a chart, with the kind permission of the AIC Group, to illustrate this point.

Let's pretend for a moment that you and two other friends invested in 3 different, but typical investments........

Friend #1 - puts $10,000 into a GIC or term deposit paying 12% in interest, and is somehow able to get that rate locked in for a 20 year period (I realize that 12% these days is pie in the sky, but bear with me for this example).

AIC Group of Funds

The Tax Advantage of a Buy & Hold Investment Philosophy

Investment Horizon	Before Tax Value of Investment	Mutual Fund with Buy & Hold Philosophy		Mutual Fund with Trading Strategy		GIC Investment	
		Terminal Value of Tax Payments	After-Tax Value of Investment	Compounded Value of Tax Payments	After-Tax Value of Investment	Compounded Value of Tax Payments	After-Tax Value of Investment
End of Year 1	$ 11,200	$ 477	$ 10,723	$ 477	$ 10,723	$ 636	$ 10,564
End of Year 2	12,544	1,011	11,533	1,043	11,501	1,384	11,160
End of Year 3	14,050	1,610	12,440	1,712	12,337	2,260	11,789
End of Year 4	15,735	2,280	13,455	2,499	13,236	3,281	12,454
End of Year 5	17,623	3,030	14,593	3,420	14,203	4,467	13,157
End of Year 6	19,738	3,871	15,867	4,494	15,244	5,840	13,899
End of Year 7	22,106	4,812	17,294	5,744	16,363	7,424	14,682
End of Year 8	24,760	5,867	18,893	7,194	17,566	9,249	15,511
End of Year 9	27,731	7,048	20,683	8,871	18,860	11,345	16,385
End of Year 10	31,059	8,371	22,688	10,807	20,252	13,749	17,309
End of Year 11	34,785	9,852	24,933	13,037	21,748	16,500	18,286
End of Year 12	38,960	11,512	27,448	15,602	23,358	19,643	19,317*
End of Year 13	43,635	13,370	30,265	18,545	25,089	23,228	20,407
End of Year 14	48,871	15,451	33,420	21,920	26,951	27,314	21,577
End of Year 15	54,735	17,782	36,953	25,782	28,954	31,962	22,773
End of Year 16	61,304	20,393	40,911	30,196	31,108	37,246	24,058
End of Year 17	68,661	23,318	45,343	35,237	33,424*	43,246	25,415
End of Year 18	76,900	26,593	50,307	40,985	35,915	50,052	26,848
End of Year 19	86,128	30,261	55,867	47,534	38,594	57,765	28,362
End of Year 20	96,463	34,369	62,094	54,988	41,475	66,501	29,962

* THE COMPOUNDED VALUE OF TAX PAYMENTS NOW EXCEEDS THE AFTER-TAX VALUE OF THE INVESTMENT!

This illustration compares the after-tax value of three investments: a GIC, a mutual fund with a trading strategy, and a mutual fund with a buy and hold philosophy. All investments are assumed to return 12% per annum before taxes which are calculated at a marginal rate of 53%. Over the 20 year horizon of these investments all distributions of income and/or capital gains are assumed to be generated at year-end and are re-invested net of taxes. It is assumed that all GIC returns are in the form of income while all mutual fund returns are in the form of capital gains. In the case of the mutual fund with the trading strategy it is assumed that there are annual distributions of 10%. The graph (over) and the table (above) are used only to reflect after-tax returns and compound growth rates. It is not intended to reflect the future value of the mutual funds or the return on investment in the mutual funds. Unit values and investment returns of mutual funds will fluctuate while the investment return of a GIC is guaranteed. Important information about AIC Mutual Funds is contained in the simplified prospectus. To obtain a copy from AIC Limited please call 1-800-263-2144 or an authorized dealer and read it carefully before investing.

Friend #2 - puts $10,000 into an actively managed equity/growth type of mutual fund that has a trading style of money-management. In other words, the investments inside the fund are bought and sold frequently. We'll also assume that this mutual fund pays out an annual distribution that is quite large, say 10%, but also earns a total rate of return of 12%, including dividends, over the same 20 year period.

You - put $10,000 into a mutual fund that concentrates solely on buying and holding good solid equity investments, but has a passive investment style. In other words, very little buying and selling takes place inside this fund. Let's also assume a 12%, 20 year average compounded rate of return on this fund.

Despite the fact that each investment has earned the same 12% pre-tax return, you'll see by the accompanying chart that the buy and hold investment strategy wins hands down versus the two other strategies. In fact, about 50% more wealth has been created, after taxes.

Because of the way the Canadian tax laws are set up, the "buy and hold" investment strategy that I favour has an important and often overlooked advantage compared to a much more "active" or "trading" approach.

An even more extreme example, (taken from AIC's Semi-Annual Report as of June 30, 1996) will help me drive this point home even more so. Imagine, for a moment, that you had only $1 to invest, which you put into an investment that grew by 100% (doubled) by year-end and then you sold it. Let's also imagine that you took the after-tax proceeds (let's assume a 39% capital gains tax rate for a moment) and were astute or lucky enough to be able to pick another investment that would double and be sold again by next year's year-end. If we repeated this process over and over again for a total of 20 years, at the end of the

20 year period, the 39% capital gains tax that you would have paid annually on the handsome profits from each sale, would have delivered approximately $8,750 to the government via taxes, and would have left you with about $13,700. Pretty good eh? If however, you had the fortunate luck of making a single spectacular investment that itself doubled annually, and did so every year for 20 years without being sold, your one dollar would have grown to an amazing $1,048,576 pre-tax value. Let's assume you then finally sold it, and paid the $408,950 ($1,048,576 X 39% capital gains tax rate) in taxes, you would be left with about $639,630. Hopefully its becoming obvious to you how the deferring of tax payments, and an investment strategy that incorporates this buy and hold style, produces a significantly larger amount of wealth to this type of investor.

By carefully selecting high quality and diversified investments and holding them for the long-term, we, as investors are able to defer taxes and utilize what would normally be paid to the government each year to produce more wealth for us and our families longer-term.

Thane Stenner is a Senior Vice President, Director & Financial Advisor with the White Rock/South Surrey office of Midland Walwyn, Canada's largest independent investment dealer serving the individual investor. Any questions may be directed to his office by calling (604) 531-8888, or by faxing (604) 531-6666.

Thane Stenner is Midland Walwyn's #1 ranked Financial Advisor in Canada. He is also a Senior Vice President and Director. He currently manages close to $200 million on behalf of his clientele from his

White Rock, British Columbia branch office. Thane has been an avid investor from a very young age and patterns his investment philosophy after the likes of Sir John Templeton of the Templeton Group, Warren Buffet of Berkshire Hathaway, and Peter Lynch of Fidelity. Because of Thane's depth of knowledge on investment and financial issues, he is used frequently by the media to comment on various financial and investment topics. Mr. Stenner has built a reputation within the financial services industry as one who has helped many Canadians build wealth and long-term security.

Is Market-Timing Worth Your Time?
By Bill Sterling

"October. This is one of the peculiarly dangerous months to speculate in stocks. The others are July, January, September, April, November, May, March, June, December, August, and February."

- Mark Twain

When fall arrives, kids are back in school. A chill is in the air. Leaves are getting ready to put on their annual colourfest. The morbid among us will be contemplating their mortality more than usual. Even the young and carefree will be dressing up as skeletons and ghosts and thinking of things that go bump in the night. And it's the season when stock prices often fall, sometimes by a lot.

That's a fact. Think of October 1929. Or October 1987. Academic studies have shown that October produces a grossly disproportionate share of large stock price declines, as does the fall season generally. Since 1885, furthermore, more than 60% of U.S. equities' days with large price declines have occurred in the last four months of the year.

So it must be time to head for the hills, right? Wrong. Those of us who make a living dissecting the wriggles and waggles of the financial markets may well want to pay some attention to seasonal influences on the markets. But for the average investor (and most above-average investors as well), we would argue that market-timing by seasonal or other factors is probably just not worth the effort.

In the first place, the seasonal studies are based on averages, which we all know can be quite misleading (think of the famous statistician whose head was frozen and whose feet were hot but, on average, felt just fine). On average, September has been the worst month for equity markets around the world, not October. But in 1996, September was a fine month, with the U.S. market rising almost 4%. Historically, July has been a good month on average, however in 1996, it was awful.

Truth be told, even if the fall is typically a weak period for stocks, there is little most investors can look at to know whether this fall will be typical or the exception that proves the rule. Sure, there are a lot of fancy indicators that we use to try to help us reach a conclusion, but we are generally happy if they are right 60% of the time. Statistically, that should be enough to give us some kind of edge on our competitors. But it still leaves us with egg on our faces 40% of the time.

Steady Eddie vs. Fearful Fred

To illustrate why the average investor should not worry too much about timing the market, we've concocted a fictional account of several very different investors and how their strategies would have worked out over time. First, let's introduce our cast of characters (any resemblance to actual persons is purely coincidental):

Cast of Characters

Steady Eddie	No rocket scientist, but lots of common sense and discipline.
Fearful Fred	Cerebral procrastinator. Reads a lot. Afraid to act.
Clever Polly	Intense. Focused. Analytical and highly disciplined. Perfect market-timer.
Hapless Hank	Obsessive about markets. Impulsive and less disciplined. Terrible market-timer.

Our story begins in January 1970, when all of our characters started to work for a living. All of them thought it was a good idea to start some kind of savings program and they all made it their objective to sock away $1,000 per year for the future.

Steady Eddie follows the "keep it simple, stupid" approach. His uncle told him that stocks are the best investment for the long term and that no one is smart enough to time the market. He recommends that Eddie put a fixed amount in the market every month and then not worry about it. "Just do it!" he tells Eddie. "That way you can concentrate on your running shoe business." So Eddie sets up a routine of monthly investing (1/12 of $1,000 every month) in a fund that does a good job of keeping pace with the Toronto Stock Exchange index over time.

Oil crises and brutal recessions come and go. Inflation and interest rates go crazy for a while. Market gurus routinely predict the end of the financial world as we know it. Real estate goes up explosively for a while and then collapses. Banks nearly go bust as their loans go sour. Mideast conflicts start, subside, and restart. Month after month, Eddie keeps investing and pays attention to his business. 26 years later, in January 1996, Steady Eddie's investment pool has grown to a healthy $78,600 through compounding. For simplicity, we'll ignore taxes (as Eddie surely would like to). [In recent years, by the way, that has become a reasonable assumption, since Canada's RRSP program is a great way for investors like Eddie to defer taxes on their investment returns.]

Fearful Fred is the cerebral type. He reads a lot about the markets and the economy and, frankly, it makes him nervous. A procrastinator by nature, he decides to keep his money in T-bills in the early 1970s as interest rates skyrocket and the stock market plummets. His risk aversion makes him natural prey for the steady stream of financial doomsters who preach that "cash is king". His motto is "better safe than sorry", and he derives satisfaction from the occasional violent market downswings that reinforce his belief in the safety of T-bills. After 26 years, Fred's investment pool has grown to only $34,610. That, too, ignores taxes. Admittedly, this latter point might make Fred a little uncomfortable, now that he's worked his way up the ladder at Revenue Canada.

Clever Polly vs. Hapless Hank

Clever Polly was a straight-A student in school and has always been intensely competitive. When she began her investment plan, she did an enormous amount of homework. She won't divulge her secrets, but she's become a truly great market-timer. Unlike Steady Eddie, who invested a fixed amount of money each month, Clever Polly's research allowed her to time her investments so that she got her $1,000 in the market annually at a price very close to the low for the year. While no one can be expected to get the best daily price of the year, Clever Polly, investing only on the last day of the month, was able to pick the best month to invest in, year after year.

After 26 years, ignoring taxes, Polly's nest egg grew to $86,950, modestly ahead of Steady Eddie's $78,600. Of course, as a chartered accountant, Clever Polly got into the RRSP game early on, so the assumption of no taxes is reasonable in recent years. Naturally, Polly is maxing out her yearly contribution

HYPOTHETICAL INVESTMENTS RESULTS:
$1,000 PER YEAR, JANUARY 1970 - JANUARY 1996 ($C)*

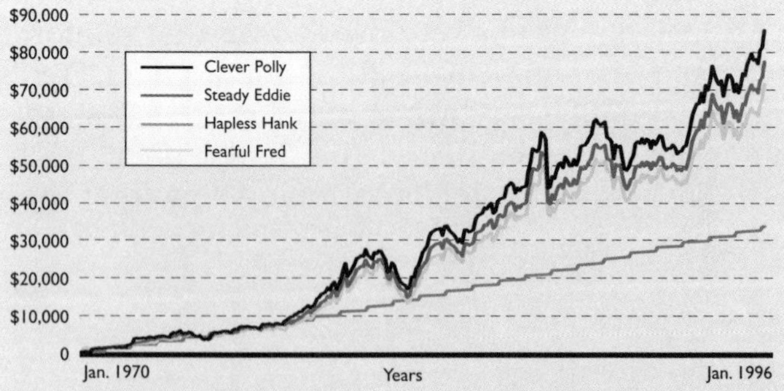

*Assumes equity returns match the relevant market index (TSE300, etc.) over the time period.

limit of $13,500 in a variety of other accounts. In fact, she is currently making a career shift to financial planning and is hoping her good investment performance will give her a shot at managing some of Steady Eddie's burgeoning fortune from his running shoe business.

Compared to Clever Polly, Hapless Hank was equally obsessive regarding his investment program, but whether it was his impulsive nature or just bad luck, he was never able to get his market-timing right. Like Polly, Hank tried each year to pick the best month of the year to invest in, and invested his $1,000 at the end of that month. Unlike Polly, however, Hank ended up picking exactly the worst month to invest in, year after year. By virtue of being in the market all those years, he still had a respectable nest egg of $72,558 (ignoring taxes), so he couldn't feel too bad. Still, relative to other market-timers, his track record was poor enough that his financial newsletter business was floundering. In fact, he was hoping to sign up Clever Polly as a business partner and leverage her guru-like results.

It's Not Whether You Win Or Lose...

The nearby graph shows how the investment programs of our four cast members fared over time. Not surprisingly, what stands out is how well our three equity investors (Eddie, Polly, and Hank) have done over time compared to Fred's results with "safe" government T-bills. All of our equity investors, even Hapless Hank, are well on their way to buying a nice condo in Florida with their investment proceeds. Meanwhile, poor Fred will be lucky to afford a trailer home. The moral of the story appears to be, "It's not whether you win or lose, it's whether you play the game at all".

To be sure, there is no guarantee that equity markets will continue to outperform T-bills to the same extent over the next thirty years. We note for reference that, since 1871, U.S. equities have outperformed T-bills 99% of the time over 20-year holding periods and 100% of the time over 30-year holding periods. Even over shorter holding periods of 5 to 10 years, equities have historically outperformed T-bills 75% to 85% of the time. So the odds are stacked against Fearful Fred.

Hypothetical Investments Results: $1,000 per year, January 1970 - January 1996*

INVESTOR

Account Value-January 1996 ($C)

	Clever Polly	Steady Eddie	Hapless Hank	Fearful Fred
Canadian Stocks (TSE 300)	86,950	78,600	72,650	—
U.S. Stocks (S&P 500)	151,140	141,610	131,060	—
Global Stocks (MSCI World)	163,810	148,800	147,740	—
Canadian T-bills	—	—	—	34,610

*Assumes equity returns match the relevant market index (TSE300, etc.) over the time period.

There are two other twists to our story that are worth pointing out. First, for those who are always afraid that "this may not be the right time to invest", Hapless Hank's experience should be reassuring. Even by investing at the worst time every year, his long-term returns were respectable and far better than if he had stayed put in T-bills.

Second, for those who don't have the time to watch every wiggle and waggle in the markets, Steady Eddie's experience should be equally reassuring. With virtually no effort at all, his strategy of "dollar cost averaging" paid off handsomely. Not only did it beat Hank's time-consuming and poorly timed efforts, but it also came quite close to Polly's results. Considering how much of Eddie's personal time it freed up, it may well have been the best overall strategy.

Finally, we have also shown how much each of our equity investors would have earned, with the same strategy and good or bad timing, had they invested in funds that matched the U.S. equity market or Morgan Stanley Capital International's World equity index (see Table 1). As is evident from the results, the risk-reward ratio for investing only in Canada has historically been considerably worse than investing in the U.S. or world equity markets. That's not surprising. Since Canada represents only about 2% of the market capitalization of world markets, an investor who targeted only Canadian equities is essentially forgoing 98% of the world's equity investment opportunities.

Had Hapless Hank invested primarily in global markets, even with his poor timing he still would have beaten Clever Polly's Canada-only results, with $147,740 after 26 years compared to Polly's Canada-only result of $86,950. Revised moral of the story, "It's not whether you win or lose, but what game you choose to play". Our recommendation: go global. And don't let anyone put ghosts in your attic about when is the right time to invest. The easy answer is now, and next month, and the month after that.

Why Baby Boomers Should Take Advantage of Emerging Markets By Neil Murdoch

In Canada, much has been written about the economic and social effects of the baby boom. Yet another, equally important, trend is taking place. Over the next twenty-five years the world will see the biggest shift in economic strength in more than a century. Today the so-called industrial economies dominate the globe, as they have for the past 150 years or so. Yet, within a generation, several are likely to be dwarfed by newly emerging economic giants. World Bank projections indicate that by the year 2020 China will be the world's largest economy. Seven of the world's top ten economies will be what are currently categorized as developing countries including Indonesia, South Korea and Thailand.

What does this shift mean for Baby Boomers? Simply put, an opportunity to participate in the long-term growth of developing countries. As a generation, we are going to live longer and retire earlier. Through the power of compounding, an extra 6% growth per annum over 20 years can more than triple the amount you have at retirement. As Baby Boomers, we still have the luxury of taking a long-term approach to planning for our retirement. Emerging markets are the fastest growing areas in the world. By investing carefully, one can find businesses operating in these tremendous macro environments that are generating fantastic returns for shareholders. A successful investor in this area, like any other, focuses on the long-term creation of value by the businesses. He/she will ignore the short-term fluctuations of the stock market. The key is to view yourself as being a silent partner in the business itself not as the purchaser of a piece of paper whose value fluctuates on a daily basis. Emerging markets are less efficient than in North America and a focus on business fundamentals will be well rewarded. Stock market fluctuations must be used as buying opportunities.

How does this shift translate into investment opportunities? There are many well-known examples such as the prediction that the Chinese government will add 140 million phones in the next six years, which is the equivalent of a new U.S. Baby Bell every two years. Also, more than $45 billion of investments will be required every year to meet Asia's power generation needs in the next decade; but it is helpful to take the process down to specific countries and companies. Ideas that we, as investors, can understand and act upon. The economic environment for creating wealth in emerging markets is astounding. For example, Malaysia has experienced GDP growth of greater than 8% per annum for each of the last eight years, while also maintaining a budgetary surplus, inflation under 4%, an appreciating currency and an unemployment rate of under 2%. As well, South Koreans consider themselves to be in the midst of a recession because their growth is slowing down this year to approximately 7%. Compare this to Canada, where we consider GDP growth of 3-4% per annum to be a boom year, our unemployment rate currently stands at 9.8%, the Canadian dollar has depreciated significantly over the last decade and, despite recent improvements, we have managed to accrue an incredible amount of debt at the federal and provincial levels.

There are certain sectors that have strong long-term secular growth trends and the ability to leverage the explosive growth in emerging market economies. Financial services, consumer products, telecommunications and infrastructure are good examples. Within financial services, certain key long-term fundamentals make insurance a strong growth area. The increasing accumulation of wealth in developing countries has caused individuals to seek ways to preserve their gains. Insurance, both life and general, allows them to do this. Insurance is also an efficient savings vehicle, an important consideration in many Asian countries. Around the world there is a very strong correlation between level of per capita income and the penetration of insurance products. As developing countries become wealthier, the insurance industry can grow at phenomenal rates. Two examples of this growth are Malaysia Assurance Alliance and Samsung Fire and Marine Insurance of Korea. Over the last three years their net profits have grown by 88% and 30% per annum respectively.

The development of a sizable middle class is another powerful trend in emerging markets. Its growth not only drives the insurance industry and other financial services as noted above, but also consumer products. They are now able to afford the "luxuries" of life such as brand-name products. Companies with strong franchises, who have successfully differentiated their products are benefiting from this trend. HM Sampoerna, an Indonesian company is benefiting from this trend. They have created a very strong brand, Dji Sam Soe, which has grown its market share despite strong competition from leading multinationals. As a result they are generating shareholder wealth at a strong pace (32% return on equity) with a net profit growth of 86% per annum over the last three years.

A modern market economy has certain basic infrastructure needs that governments around the world have realized are best satisfied through the private sector. These needs include roads, power utilities, homes and office buildings. Construction companies present a direct method to participate in this boom. Gamuda Berhad, one of the largest construction companies in Malaysia, has taken advantage of the opportunities presented by the tremendous growth in the Malaysian economy. Over the last three years their revenues and profits have both grown by 43% per annum. They have also taken advantage of privatization opportunities by winning concessions to build and operate toll roads. By the year 2000 almost 50% of their profits will come from collecting tolls, a steady, low risk business.

The telecommunications sector has strong projected growth rates due to economic expansion, low historical usage rates caused by past inefficiencies of state owned companies, new technologies and deregulation. The opportunities in this area span the spectrum from recently privatized monopolies such as Telefonica del Peru to wireless companies such as Korea Mobile Telecom ("KMT"). Peru has only 5 telephone lines per hundred people versus 56 for Canada. They have almost doubled their lines in use in the last three years and expect to almost double them again in the next three years. Profits have also boomed with an increase of 90% per annum during the same period. KMT is an example of the success that wireless companies are having in developing countries. The company with over 2.5 million subscribers, has had incredible growth in its customer base, averaging over 82% per annum in the last three years. They have been extremely profitable during this growth, recording a net profit of $233 million U.S. in 1995, while most wireless companies in North America are just becoming profitable.

Emerging markets combine the excitement of growth with the opportunities of change as the people of developing countries aspire and drive for improved economic, social and political standards. Governments are adopting free market principles, opening up their economies to trade, privatizing, deregulating and attracting capital equity. These changes are the stimulants for economic growth and the creation of vibrant equity markets. Wealth is being created in these countries at a fabulous rate.

The above discussion attempts to provide a brief glimpse of opportunities. The secret to successful investing in emerging markets is to focus on the reason for investing initially, long-term growth. If the fundamentals for growth in the economy and in particular businesses are still in place then any gyrations in the stock market should be treated as buying opportunities. As Baby Boomers, we have the benefit of being able to take a long-term perspective and, over time, stock markets have proven remarkably adept at recognizing the creation of shareholder wealth in the real world. One of the best ways to ensure that we, as Baby Boomers, have a long and enjoyable retirement is to take advantage of this fantastic opportunity.

Neil Murdoch, 36, is part of the three man money management team at AIC. His focus is on international investing. He has been involved in the purchase and sale of businesses in the international area for the past eight years. Mr. Murdoch has an MBA from Northwestern University and a law degree from the University of Toronto. AIC Group of Funds, with over $1 billion in assets under management, has been creating portfolios of excellent businesses since 1985.

The Case For High Yield Bond Funds
By Sue Dabarno

We have seen mutual fund assets grow to 175 billion in mid '96. Canadian consumers' expectations for product choice demand that all mutual fund families ensure that their unit holders have access to a diversified product line that will include:

1. A variety of different and growing "gateways" to gain access to product information.

2. Qualified personal advisors to assist in selecting the mutual fund best suited to meet investor needs.

3. On-going assistance in educating the investor on products, fees and performance.

4. New product innovations that indicate a fund family is attuned to the changing marketplace.

The "Atlas" family of funds respects all those investor needs and is committed to a delivery of information that "will make the world more manageable than you think". We want to make it easy to diversify investments and have confidence that Atlas will provide new innovations designed to match client needs with marketplace changes. The case for High Yield Bond Funds is an example of such a strategy.

Facts About Corporate Debt In Canada

- The credit spectrum is divided into 7 parts ranging from highest quality to lowest quality. The credit ratings are AAA, AA, A, BBB, BB, B and CCC.

- A High Yield strategy concentrates on companies rated BBB or lower.

- Over 70% of the TSE 300 companies would be rated BBB or lower if all companies had publicly available credit ratings. In fact, many are rated in this manner, purely due to the cyclical nature of their business.

- High yield debt is analyzed for investment by focusing on the credit outlook for the company, ie., the risk and the incremental return as measured by the yield spread over federal government bonds of the same maturity. These parameters allow investors to evaluate the risk/reward relationship between higher yielding corporate debt and "credit risk-free" federal government obligations. Over the last two decades these benchmarks reveal a premium of 200 to 400 basis points paid by higher-yielding corporate bonds.

The Case For Investing In High Yield Bonds

- High yield corporate debt can serve two fundamental needs of more traditional fixed income and equity investors: enhanced returns through higher income or improved risk management through broader diversification. Relative to the full spectrum of choices for the fixed income investor, performance is enhanced by participating in high yield bonds.

- Investing in high yield bonds can lower overall portfolio risk for a given level of expected return. This is because high yield bonds have significantly different risk and return characteristics from high grade bond and equities. In fact, SEI Capital Markets Research in the U.S. concluded that, "Investors with commitments to both fixed income and equity should include high yield bonds in their portfolios to obtain further diversification benefits. The target allocation to high-yield bonds should be between 10% and 30% of the fixed income allocation."

When To Consider High Yield Bonds

- Diversification within the high yield bond asset class is paramount. Diversification means owning at least 10 bonds spread across different industries.

- For many retail investors the best way to invest in high yield bonds is through a good mutual fund where you pay an experienced manager to manage and diversify credit risk.

Investor Needs Are Met With High Yield Bond Funds

- Investors with commitments to fixed income and equity should add high yield bond funds for diversification benefits.

- High yield allocations should be made from fixed income rather than equity.

- Diversification of domestic fixed income portfolio is achieved through corporate bonds for interest rate risk reduction and yield enhancement.

- High Yield Bond Fund complements an existing domestic fixed income portfolio concentrated in government and provincial debt.

- Investors take advantage of the higher long term total return of corporate bonds through a diversified and professionally managed portfolio.

Sue Dabarno is President of Atlas Capital Group. Sue joined Atlas from Canada Trust where she worked in many diversified senior positions over the last 20 years, including regional branch operations and product management. Sue was responsible, at Canada Trust, for the launch and growth of Everest Mutual Funds. Assisting Sue with this article was Doug Knight, fixed income manager of Deons-Knight Capital Management Ltd. and the manager of the Atlas High Yield Bond portfolio.

A LAST WORD...

Recently I was enjoying a plate of 25¢ chicken wings in Etobicoke, Ontario. (While my editor was slaving over a lap-top in a stuffy office on a long weekend). As I was eating and penning these final words, I noticed a sign promoting "Laser Karaoke" every Thursday evening. Admittedly, with three small children, my wife Tracy and I do not get out as often as we once did and thus I am rather sheltered. To be sure, I have certainly heard of and participated in an evening of Karaoke, much to the dismay of my friends. Where the very nature of Karaoke is concerned, one of these aforementioned friends maintains that the machines should come with instructions that read, "just add alcohol!" As someone who, for the most part, abstains from alcohol, I have both sung and listened to others while sober. Thus it goes without saying, I avoid Karaoke whenever possible! Regardless, this idea of "Laser" Karaoke piqued my curiosity to the point where I was compelled to seek clarification from my waiter. Fully anticipating a response detailing strobe lights and laser light shows, I was unprepared for the waiter's reply. Indeed, what followed my inquiry was a thorough explanation about how the sound quality was superior, the words were easier to read because they were on a big screen and that ultimately this technology was designed to help one perform better. Thus my next question was, "With all of this superior sound and technology, what happens if you do not have a good voice?" His reply? "We boo."

Investing for the Baby Boomer is in keeping with

this anecdote. Indeed, in the next five years you may read twenty financial books, and countless daily financial newspapers. You may also become a seminar junkie and effectively know "everything". However, without making a commitment and an investment in your financial future, you lose. Remember in the business of creating wealth, only applied knowledge is power. I do not consider myself a motivator, and that is certainly not the purpose of this book. Instead, my aim is to give you a working knowledge of what the Baby Boomer must understand in order to be financially successful. You do not need to become a financial advisor to succeed because you can delegate this work.

In First Lady Hilary Clinton's speeches and in her book, she eloquently brings forth a concept that is vitally important in raising successful children in the nineties. Her argument is that a child's development is clearly the responsibility of his or her parents or guardians. Supporting the parents, however, is a network of community teachers, coaches, neighbours, doctors; and business people. In essence, "it takes a village."

Regardless of whether it may be raising our children, examining new ideas in cancer research, creating successful business or building wealth, I believe this idea is one that can impact powerfully in many aspects of our lives. As a client you need an outstanding financial advisor, an accountant, an investment research team, a strong firm and money managers who can lower risk and increase returns. Supporting this team, you need people who can provide financial information in newspapers, and on the internet. In other words, to be a successful investor, "it takes a village." Please do not sell yourself short. As a Baby Boomer who may be just a few short years from educating children or even retirement, the decisions you make today are extremely important and as such must be well thought-out. The market does not recognize "nice people" nor does it understand the fact that you have worked hard and are deserving of wealth. Financial markets only reward good decisions, thus you must continue to learn and exercise patience.

We are Baby Boomers! Our peers include Bill Gates, Wayne Gretzky, Oprah Winfrey and U.S. President, Bill Clinton. We understand and revel in technology, higher education and the love of recreation, family and balance. As a generation, the Boomers have already secured a place in history as an innovative, successful group of men and women. Despite these achievements, we are feeling the financial pressure of higher living and increased costs. Moreover, to a certain extent we have become too dependent on large corporations and big government. As individuals, we must take the initiative and change. If you have already changed and have begun to build wealth, congratulations! If you have not, start now. Irrespective of where you are now, remember to invest long-term and see volatility and change in financial markets as your opportunity to "bargain hunt" for great, undervalued investments. Invest as a contrarian and use the indecision of others (who are less informed) to buy low cost investments for your portfolio. Above all else, always keep a "cool head" and begin to build wealth now.

The Blue Jays are twenty years-old.

The clock is ticking.

"When written in Chinese, the word crisis is composed of two characters – one represents danger and the other represents opportunity."

John F. Kennedy